The Last Hunt in Early County

The Last Hunt in Early County

John C. Blythe

To order additional copies of this book, contact:
Xlibris Corporation
1-888-795-4274
www.Xlibris.com
Orders@Xlibris.com
66416

Contents

Dedication

This book is dedicated to the memory of William and to the memory of all the setters and pointers who sleep under the dogwood tree in our yard, and to my hunting buddies Paul and Toby. The book is for Ruth who "set my spirit free," and encouraged me to tell the stories for our children and grandchildren.

Introduction

Telling the story and keeping it interesting is problematic for an old doc like me. I believe my medical background is partially to blame. The years of reading bland, scientific medical literature and writing the same traditional, mentally templated, dull reports have blighted and dimmed my keener senses of description. Doctors have been imprinted to report things objectively and to use precise descriptive terms, "medical words." This is not conducive to good writing, and it makes for dull reading; I know that. I have tried to make the stories of the hunts interesting, but I have not embellished them. In telling the stories I have been subjective, have told them from my perspective, but the stories are true, all of them. Paul might disagree with some of the details, but this is the way that I remember them. There is no mendacity here.

Another difficulty is that the humor and the pathos of situations, the inflections of the voices, the rhythms and pauses of conversation are difficult to reproduce on the written page. So much of life's experiences are ephemeral, lasting but a moment and vanishing as the laughter fades, and the nuance of the moment becomes lost, leaving not simply a memory but a feeling. There is, for example, the thing about a covey rise, the clamor and flutter and roar of wings flailing when quail erupt in a blur, which I cannot put into words. It is beyond the reach of my vocabulary, and for that matter, I have never read it adequately described.

There is this saying that "if everyone else climbed a tree, he would dig a hole," and I am tempted to use it in describing Paul, but he is not that way, not really. He is set in his ways, to be sure, and conservative—conservative the way a lot of good ole boys in the Deep South are conservative. At one time I was, too. Deep fried Southern Baptists don't drink alcohol, not as a rule. At least some don't. It was certainly ingrained in us in the middle of the last century that drinking is wrong. While all Southern Baptist deacons vow to "abstain from the sale and consumption of alcoholic beverages," some actually take the vow seriously. Paul does and is not hypocritical about it. He promised not to drink alcohol, and he doesn't. He is no prude; he just always tries to do right, and I have always admired him for that. By the same token, it makes him subject to occasional friendly ribbing. It is my contention, however, that it is his idiosyncrasies that account for most of the grief inflicted on him.

There is a lot of sunshine in Alabama. Most of us enjoyed the sun when we were young, getting a nice tan and burning a few times each summer. Later when we learned that getting roasted wasn't all that good for us, we became more careful. Some of us became extremely careful, Paul in particular. Many in his family lived to be old, really old, like over a hundred. Skin has to last a long time when you live to be that old, he explained, and he was always in possession of sunscreen. He spent an inordinate amount of time lathing it on the unprotected parts of his body in case he should enjoy the family longevity. I became more nonchalant about the sun after developing prostate cancer.

I was accustomed to Paul's ways, and he to mine. We had been friends since childhood, and he was always the one most likely to go bird hunting with me even when the prospects were dismal. Each enjoyed the other's company, and we dreamed of the day when we would go some place where there are plenty of birds and both of us would limit out.

Paul and I were not spring chickens when we first began the annual February trips to Early County. Paul and William were fifty-five, and I was a pip of a lad at fifty-three. Actually, that seems young now.

It is hard to say exactly what it is that makes friendships develop or what bonds you to someone whom you are only with three days once a year. I suspect it is in part the things that we share—the common interest, the adventure, the laughter and the pain. There are a lot of men whom I respect and even love, but thinking on it, there are probably only a score whose friendship I truly venerate.

I took a liking to William from the get-go, and I cannot imagine anyone not liking him. Although he lived in a very rural area and had no close neighbors, William did not lack for friends. Toby and his family lived a mile away and were the closest white family. There were still a few, a very few, colored families that lived within a mile—the reminder of a way of life long passed. They lived in the same small houses that they had occupied for decades, and some still farmed a little and had yard chickens and a hog or two. I do not recall seeing any young children around those home places. It was the end of an era, just past the transition from another world. We occasionally talked of it, but not for long because there was a melancholy sadness about its passing. I was fortunate to be a witness to the old way of life—to dirt farming and clawing out an existence and sweating and to making it one more year, maybe. But the Soil Bank, and Social Security and Welfare finally drove a stake through the heart of the Old South. William "drew a check," and he got by. Surely the allotments and the payments not to plant crops and the payments to plant pine trees were enough to keep the wolves away from his door. He drove an old Mercury Cougar, and he had an old truck that did not run, at least I never saw it run. He wore old work clothes and occasionally some briar pants and a pair of worn boots, but maybe that was just what he wanted to wear. Certainly in no way was he pretentious; what you see is what you get. He was not a sybarite, not a person devoted to luxury. On the contrary, he liked simple pleasures and he enjoyed them with unrestrained gusto, consequently it was delightful to be in his presence. He tolerated his ailments with quiet reserve, patience, and privacy but could not hide his concern for mine.

I am not sure how he and Toby became friends. Maybe it was because they were mile-away-next-door-neighbors. Maybe it began in "choir practice." They were hunting and fishing "partners," the same as Paul and I. Toby was thirty years younger than we, about the age of my boys; however, he fit right in the same as either of them would have, and in that regard I understand the pleasure of a sprite young grig. Toby is as unique as William or Paul, or even me, and he is, to borrow a Nash Buckingham phrase, "de shootingest gent'man" I've ever known.

My grandfather had been a vegetable peddler and small farmer up near Reynolds, Georgia, out of the plantation area. I never knew him, and know very little about him, but for some reason I have a niggling feeling that I have unknown kinfolk in Georgia. I occasionally get a lump of homesickness in my throat just riding around the back roads of Early County.

William said that there weren't nearly as many quail as there used to be. He told all sorts of stories to illustrate his point. But compared to what we were used to in Central Alabama, the hunting was good. Most of the coveys were large even in February, and we managed to take some birds home nearly every time. We would have taken a lot more had we "shot the misses out of our guns," as William facetiously recommended.

I

The Last Hunt in Early County

The anticipation of another hunting trip to South Georgia always disturbs my sleep. The years have slowed my step and increased the fatigue of an all-day quail hunting trip, but have not dulled the anticipation. I can't help it; I get that little boy excitement the night before and am so keyed up that sleep comes fitfully and hardly at all.

I had a feeling that this year it would be different, and my anticipation was flavored with a hint of melancholy and now and then with a vague uneasy sense of sadness. But the routine of preparation and the recollection of past days afield overwhelmed me subliminally with unsuppressed joy.

The rain began at sundown Thursday. A cold front was predicted to pass by mid—morning on Friday, proceeding from west to east as usual. Paul and I had been keeping up with the weather and had discussed it several times as we made final plans for the trip.

Our house is heavily insulated, so it takes a heavy rain to be heard, but I knew that it was raining even though I couldn't hear it, and I sensed that it was getting cold. Sleep had come with unusual ease that night, but when I awakened for the routine early morning toilet walk, I began to think about Early County, quail and William. I tried not to thrash around and awaken Ruth, and I tried to go back to sleep realizing that the trip takes more out of me each year. Apparently I did go back to sleep, because when I sleep on my good ear I do not hear the alarm sounding. Ruth nudged me, "The alarm."

I've never been a morning person anyway; getting out of bed has always been difficult, especially in the winter, and especially when it's raining. It's just hard to leave the comforts of a warm bed and soft arms.

I felt her nudge me. "Are you awake?"

"I think the Sleep Monster has got me," I muttered, admitting that I had drifted back to the balmy land of somnambulant bliss.

"Better get up if you are going hunting."

I eased from confines of her arms with great ambivalence and stumbled to the laundry room to let the dogs out. Ruth insisted that they sleep inside when it is cold, and of course Sludge, our faithful lab, had to be inside any time it rained. I was greeted by the sulfurous "green fog" and by the surprised-looking dogs all obviously wondering why they had to go out so early. When I opened the door I could see the sparkles of the sprinkling rain in the floodlight above the carport. I stood there for a moment to sense the temperature and thought, "If the front has come in like it should, it is not going to be all that cold."

I clicked on the coffee maker which Ruth had prepared the night before and hurried back to get dressed. I tried not to disturb her more, but as I slid into my silks, she said, "You and Paul really picked a bad weekend to go on a hunting trip."

"Don't worry, Ruthie Mae, I said, "It's going to be great! By the time we get to William's house, the front will have pushed the rain to the east. It never gets too cold in Early County, and we sure won't have to worry about snakes."

"Did you let Sludge out?"

"I'm about to," I answered as I stroked his velvet ears. Soon he had enough and ambled down the steps to join his companions.

"You know he will be frightened if it thunders."

"The rain has about stopped. I didn't hear any thunder. Did you?"

"All I heard last night was your snoring." She softened, "and I'm going to miss that tonight."

"Leave the bedroom door open and you can listen to Sludge snore," I suggested.

Sludge is the center piece of our home; that is, he lies in the center of it and sleeps most of the time. He was my birthday gift to Ruth eleven years earlier when he was only a handful of black lab puppy. Now he is a hulking 130 pound watch dog/best friend and general *bon vivant* for Ruth. He is retired form retrieving doves except on the coolest days but still fetches sticks on a part-time basis, if they are thrown in the pond. His chasing doves, the ones that he and I both had expected to fall but didn't, is hampered now in part by his obesity and in part by the creep of years. Nothing much excites him any more except for the dog bone that she faithfully gives him first thing each morning—and thunder! He has a fear of thunder. But Sludge is not feckless, not even in his old age. His purpose, his reason to be, his real worth is related to his just being a part of our home.

Ruth made out to be angry when I gave her a dog for her birthday, but one look into the pool of those dark eyes and a puppy lick on the face won her over. It was love at the first hint of puppy breath. He was her dog, and I had to ask permission to take him hunting. As he became senior dog, I had to have her permission to put him out of the house. What made him afraid of thunder is known only to him and God.

"What are you going to name him?" I ventured to ask her the day after her birthday, hoping that she would not continue to call him "Sweetie" or "Darling."

"I don't know. What is the blackest thing you can think of," she returned.

I rambled off the usual list, as she shook her head negatively with each suggestion. "What is the blackest thing you can think of?" I asked acknowledging the strain on my vocabulary.

"The blackest thing I can think of is that stuff the city is spreading on the hayfields."

"Sludge?"

"Yes, that."

"Hey, what a great name for a dog! I've never heard of a dog named Sludge! That's unique." I could barely contain my excitement.

"We're not naming my baby after . . . after . . . you-know-what!" she protested, pulling him to her face. "Not my sweet thing!"

That's how Sludge got his name, at least his first name. A few days later, Ruth was filling out an application for his papers and was puzzling about a second name. "What do you think, Zelma?" she asked her house keeper/personal advisor. "What goes with Sludge?"

"How 'bout Sludge Hammer?" came the immediate reply.

So let it be written.

I finished dressing, turned out the light in my study and eased through the bedroom as quietly as I could. My gun and bags were on the kitchen table from the night before. I poured a cup of coffee and sipped it as I laced my boots.

"John." She called sleepily from the bedroom.

"Yes?"

"You and Paul are not going to make those puppies ride in the back of the truck in this weather, are you?" I could tell that wasn't a question. And I was a little irritated that she insisted on referring to *my dogs* as "puppies."

"You don't want them to walk all the way to South Georgia, do you Ruthie Mae?" At one time it irritated her for me to call her that, but I kept reassuring her that all Southern women have double first names, and she grew to accept it as my affectionate name for her.

"Not in the truck!" This time I knew not to talk back.

"We'll just go in the Yukon then." I was beginning to wish that she had not awakened, but I knew in my heart that she was right and was secretly glad that she nixed the truck.

"Good." She sounded triumphant.

"Paul is going to bitch every time one farts," I said under my breath. I could hear her snickering in the bedroom.

Paul arrived with his usual bluster at six, or as he would say, "0600." "Doctor, are you at the ready?" That was some of his jar-head talk. Paul, a retired Marine Major and ex-confirmed bachelor is fixed like concrete in his ways. Despite twenty years of active duty, he emerged a straight-arrow, Southern Baptist conservative, non-smoker, non-drinker, and board certified anal retentive. He muttled through Auburn University in six years earning a degree in chemistry, but contrary to the non-academic image he projected, he had a steel trap mine for facts, history and trivia. He never lacked subject for conversation nor incentive to talk, even when he was the only listener. I am amazed at his knowledge of trivia and historical facts, and his discourses always make our long rides pleasurable.

We have been friends since childhood. He and my brother were two years ahead of me in school and a little less than that in actual age. Since they were best friends, we were all very close. Not being a blood brother, Paul did not disdain my tagging along as much as Al did. We experienced the same Baptist Church up bringing, the same Boy Scouts, football, and small Southern town peculiarities. More like a brother to us than a friend, he accompanied our family on vacations and was subject to my parents' reprimands and admonitions the same as we were. My children have always referred to him as "Uncle Poolie," a title he readily affirms. We began hunting together with Red Ryder BB rifles and took up real guns at age twelve or thereabout.

"Want some coffee?"

"Yes, but first I need to use the facility," he said as he closed the door to the guest toilet. Almost instantly he blustered, "Good gosh! You just peed all over the damn toilet seat. I can't believe this!" Paul usually speaks in a loud voice, and I felt sure that Ruth heard him shriek.

"Relax, Poolie," I said hoping not to disturb her more than I already had. "The dogs don't raise the lid when they drink, and they wouldn't like you sitting on their water bowl." I could hear Ruth snickering.

"Yeah. Well, they don't have to be so sloppy."

Then from the bedroom, "John, not in the truck."

"Yes mam."

"We're going to have to go in the Yukon," I reported as he emerged.

"They have already wet me down, so you tell your sorry hounds not to be passing any gas till we get to William's." He was chuckling as he poured his coffee. I was sure he thought that I had set him up with the wet toilet seat.

We put a tarp in the back of the Yukon and loaded two dog boxes, putting two dogs in each. Once we had our gear loaded, the car was almost full. We did not take Leukos this year; he had gotten too old and feeble. Even he realized it. He stood in the door watching for a while as we finished loading, then shuffled back inside and took his usual position under the kitchen table.

A word of explanation is probably needed here. At the time I had five bird dogs: Leukos, Belle, Dan, Freck, and Mae. Leukos—Leukos Canis—is the father of Dan, Freck, and Mae. None of the younger are registered, and none have second names. Belle, their mother, is registered, as is Leukos. Understand that I know to use "sire" and "dam" when discussing dogs, but these are not *just* dogs, not according to Ruth. I got Leukos, an offspring of Mr. Thor, as a pup, and I named him Leukos Canis because he is a white dog. As he grew older, I wanted to maintain his blood line, and after much negotiation talked Ruth into letting me buy a girl dog—not a bitch—for the sake of procreation, and hunting. Although I was looking for a white English setter lassie for Leukos, we found a litter of Llewellyn setters, and we could not resist a beautiful tri-colored little girl. Time passed, and after suffering through two heats with Belle in the house wearing some sort of dog sanitary napkin Ruth ordered from a catalog, we put her in the dog pin with Leukos. Belle had three pups. It was *not my* decision to keep all three of them, nor was it my decision to have Belle and Mae fixed. It was my firm decision not to have Freck and Dan fixed.

After many years of study and meditation I developed a philosophy of dog naming, maybe an "understanding" is a better word. Bird dogs should have one-syllable names. When one owns more than one dog, they should be named with different sounds so as to avoid confusing them when they are addressed. It is for that reason when I hunt Leukos, I call him "Luke." Belle and Mae are the two most common second names of Southern women, as in Ruthie Mae and Linda Belle. Dan was named for Dan Broughton, a buddy, and sometime hunting and fishing companion. Freck has freckles. I learned to name dogs the way I usually learn things—by trial and error. A good thing about getting older is that there are fewer things left to learn by trial and error.

Once I had a pointer named Millie whom I took down to Hatchechubbee, Alabama to have bred with a dog named Warhoop Dapper Jack, son of the famous Warhoop Jake. I selected two pups from the litter to keep. My children named them Beauregard and Sebastian. I suppose I could have overridden them and named them more traditional bird dog names, but I was too pleased with the Southern sounding names to object. The next fall I took Sebastian down to Hatchechubbee to Mr. Herman Smith who took dogs to Canada to train. As I was about to head home, he stopped me and asked, "By the way, Doc, what is the dog's name?"

"Sebastian."

"What?" At first I thought he did not understand me over the rumble of my pickup.

"Sebastian," I spoke louder.

"Say that again," he roared back.

"The dog's name is Sebastian." I spoke as slowly and clearly as possible after turning off the truck motor.

"Yeah, but what do you call the damn dog?"

"Sam," I answered almost before he could finish the sentence.

That evening around the dinner table I told the children that it seemed to me that the dogs should have nick names that I could use when hunting, so what did they think about "Sam" and "Beaux?"

Paul never lacks for conversation. No sooner had we loaded the dogs and closed the doors than he began to reflect on this and that. First a diatribe about dogs riding in luxury in the back of doctor's cars, then dogs in general, and concluding about the aroma of canine flatus, then he took a breath. "Poolie," I broke in indicating my disinterest in his fault-finding, "I'm glad we are going to William's again. It has always been the highlight of our bird season. I was afraid we were not going to get there this year."

"Yes," he said, becoming serious and almost religious in his tone. "But this is likely the last hunt in Early County for us."

There was a long silence as we both pondered the possible end of an era. After a while of reflecting back over the years, I broke the silence, "Seems like only yesterday that I came with you for the first time to hunt at William's . . . ."

II

First Trip to Early County

It was my first trip to Early County, Georgia to bird hunt with William Hudspeth. Paul had arranged the trip. They had been college chums and had hunted the Hudspeth lands during the five or so years they were at Auburn. Twenty years in the Marines had interrupted Paul's trips, but since his retirement he had been down a time or two. Paul told me all about the trips, hunting the edges and fencerows around the large soybean and peanut fields. It was a far cry from bird hunting in Central Alabama, not only in the terrain, but especially in the abundance of birds in South Georgia.

Both Paul and William were bachelors at the time, and both were stuck in their own brand of bachelorhood. William took delight in teasing Paul, invariably and in great detail, telling him how he would get him fixed up with some fine South Georgia woman during his visit down. Paul would always demurely say, "Now William, be kind. Be kind to the Poolie." This would only egg him on, and William would launch into a detailed description about the *kind* of woman he had in mind and the kind of *things* that she would likely expose Paul to. Paul would respond to each onslaught with, "Be kind, now." Like a puppy pestering an old cat, William continued almost from the time the truck stopped in his yard until it was loaded and headed back to Alabama. William had a sense of the absurdities of life, those things that depart from the expected or were ridiculous, and he found them humorous. His jibes at Paul were a contradiction of Paul's real world.

I was invited to join Paul for the first time in February 1993. Paul never owned a bird dog—or any dog for that matter. I was the one with the dogs and the one who usually found the hunting spot around Tallapoosa Count for us. My dogs were never all that good, mostly from lack of exposure to many quail and in part because they were trained by me. I could hardly contain my excitement at the prospect of going to some real bird hunting territory

19

and exposing my dog to enough birds to let him know what this business is about.

The preceding year was not a very good one for me. I had undergone surgery for prostate cancer in March and struggled with a long and tedious recovery. I had not missed much work and no bird hunting, but it was an effort, and I'm sure that my love for the outdoors aided in the rehabilitation process. I know that it helped me get my mind off the fact that surgery did not make me completely cancer free. So, I anticipated the trip with wonder and excitement as the chance, literally, of a lifetime. If I was ever going to do real bird hunting, now was the time.

In my mind I had pictured how things would be, but reality and imagination are always at variance, though not necessarily better or worse. William lived in the old family home built in the nineteen thirties in the country north of Blakely. It was a pleasant and ample house, but not the plantation home I had pictured. Fire a few years earlier had done some minor damage, and William had redone some of it, giving it something of an update. He mostly lived in the back bedroom and the large eat-in kitchen, also in the back of the house. The front rooms were unused except when there was "big company." As best I can tell, the front door was never locked and hardly ever used.

William kept his boat and trailer in the original carport at the side of the house next to his bedroom. He had added a new carport behind the house which covered the entrance to the kitchen and was decorated with an assortment of fishing rods, minnow buckets and boots, along with boxes of tractor parts. Under this carport on the side nearest to the house, he parked his '76 Mercury Cougar, and on the outer side there was an assortment of the usual garage stuff including a charcoal grill made from the rim of a tandem axel truck. A few yards away from the carport was his dog pen, and in the pen were two small, unimpressive female pointers. Behind the house a ways was an old windmill that once pumped water from the well. The pump house now housed a regular electric pump. To the side was an assortment of out buildings including two old barns and a long open-front equipment shed. In the shed was a John Deere tractor. Another one sat outside with an off-set disc harrow attached. His old truck sat next to the tractor in the shed. Between the house and the barn was a patch of bamboo, probably some imported variety that grew tall and thick, the kind that would make good fishing poles.

The roads in that part of Early County except for the highways were all dirt and all straight, running north-south, east-west, setting the land off in sections for the most part. They were well maintained by the county and were worked regularly with a motor grader, or as we say in Alabama, a "patrol." They were smooth as dirt roads go and were red and sandy like the soil of South Georgia. There wasn't much dust in February, usually. William's house sat just down from a crossroad and off the road about seventy-five yards.

William was a short man with sandy blond hair graying at the temples. He had a ruddy, weather beaten face that was softened by a wide grin and sparkling blue eyes. Paul had told me that he had had some health problems and had suffered since childhood with some sort of arthritis that had caused him considerable trouble getting around. As a physician, I was curious and sympathetic at his physical appearance and guessed that the arthritic deformities were caused by juvenile rheumatoid arthritis. Despite the physical problems, he seemed happy and nonchalant, and though he shuffled and limped, he seemed to be only a little uncomfortable most of the time. Clearly, he was tough and stoic and he never indicated much of an interest in discussing his health problems with me.

Before his final year of college, William's father died, so he left Auburn and returned home to run the family farm. And so, he farmed. With the help of the hired hands, who were all black and who had "been in the family" for generations, he farmed the fertile soils of Early County. He row-cropped hundreds of acres of soybeans, peanuts and cotton. He ran cattle on the bottom land along the Chattahoochee River. He raised goats and hogs and a few mules. He had bad years when it did not rain enough and bad years when it rained too much. He had some good years. He suffered the down markets and down machinery. He knew about government subsidies, set-asides, CRP and soil conservation. He knew about the Federal Land Bank and the regular bank. William was a third generation South Georgia red neck dirt farmer. He knew how to work, and he knew how to value a good worker. In addition, William was a tobacco chewing, beer drinking, good ole boy who loved to hunt and fish. He became a hero of mine from the outset.

When we arrived at William's we were greeted by a wide grin and a gusty "Hello, Sweet'n!" It soon became apparent that this endearment dated back to college days, and according to Paul, had something to do with William's being "something of a lady's man."

Paul introduced William and me, and after proper niceties, I introduced William to Leukos as I let him out to stretch and sniff. He looked at the totally white setter, a registered son of Mr. Thor, and said in his gravelly baritone, "Well, he's a pretty thing." The way he said it was clearly condescending, and I knew he meant, "I wouldn't have a setter if you gave him to me." This unspoken opinion was verbalized several times during the next two days, after William and I had broken the ice, so to speak.

Leukos was my pride. He was the last to be sold of his litter, apparently because he was a little cock-eyed. Other than that, he was a beautiful dog, essentially all white. He held his tail high and hunted hard and fast. I had actually washed him in my shower the night before, and indeed he was "a pretty thing," as William said—unless you looked him head on. I had not given any thought about how his beautiful white long hair would attract cockleburs and sand spurs like nails to a magnet.

On our way down, Paul and I stopped at a grocery store in Fort Gains and picked up some "makings," so while Paul was making sandwiches, William and I sat at the old round oak kitchen table and began getting acquainted, talking bird hunting and bird dogs. We hit it off immediately. Our serious conversations were frequently interrupted by William cutting his eyes over to Paul and saying, "Now Sweet'n, I can fix you up with one of the ladies tonight." Paul would flinch and respond, "Be kind William, we just came to hunt and enjoy your company."

We let the dogs down shortly after noon. What a day to bird hunt! It had rained several days the week before, and water still gathered in puddles. The ground was wet and slippery, and mud stuck stubbornly to our boots, collecting in layers. I kept looking for a rock to scrape the mud off, but there are few rocks in Early County, a sharp contrast to the rocky hills of home. It was a beautiful day in South Georgia, almost entirely clear skies. Paul lavishly anointed himself with sunscreen and joined William and me as we overlooked a large peanut field where we were about to hunt the edges.

"Paul, you going to the beach?" William asked as he approached.

"No. Why?"

"Well, you smell like a coconut. That's why."

"One of these days you and the Doc are going to wish you had done the same thing."

"But Paul, you're so greased up that I don't see how you hold a gun!" William looked at Paul and then at me and began to chuckle.

The hunt went well for a short while, but soon it became apparent that Leukos was more interested in the little bitch named "Blue" than he was in birds. "She's been out of heat about a week," William reassured.

"Doc, you need to explain that to your dog," Paul joked. "He thinks you got him all spick and span to go courting and not bird hunting."

"Look a-yonder. Blue is pointed." William nodded to a clump of bushes about forty yards ahead. We summoned the other dogs, and presently there was a three dog point followed by the explosion of a covey rise. I do not remember if we killed any birds on that rise, but it changed Leukos's orientation for a while, and the hunting began in earnest.

It was not long before the pride I had in my beautiful dog began to melt. Leukos kept bumping singles, refused to back and didn't even offer to retrieve. He seemed wild with excitement, running at full speed and paying no attention to my whistle or calling. Every bird he flushed seemed to only make him worse. When Leukos was not running full blast, he was sniffing and licking at Blue. We managed to kill a few birds over Liz and Blue. I missed a lot of easy shots. One of the times was near an AME church where William said there was always a covey near by. When we neared the church, we could tell that a funeral had recently ended, so we turned back through some light woods toward the Jeep. There in the open woods William's pointers found a covey of birds. When they flushed, the one I was following suddenly climbed higher and higher as if trying to get above the tall pines. I shot twice, missing both times. Somehow I just knew that William thought I was the worst bird hunter he had ever seen, and that maybe Leukos was just the kind of dog I needed.

Before long Leukos began to run out of steam. He reported in after wallering in a mud puddle, looking mostly red, and his tongue dangling from the corner of his mouth. Huffing and panting, foam drooling from his mouth, he looked more cockeyed than usual. Paul eased over by me and said loud enough for William to clearly hear, "He's a pretty thing." William stiffeled a chuckle as his huge grin seemed to reach from ear to ear.

"Doc, you want to put him in the jeep?" suggested William. "Looks like he needs a rest."

"No," I said defiantly, "what he needs is a load of number eights on his butt."

"Sounds like you're getting in a snit about your dog, "William observed, speaking more to Paul than to me.

"Aw, but Doc," chimed in Paul. "He's a pretty thing!" Paul and William bellowed with laughter.

"Yeah, I'm pretty too. Maybe that's why I can't hit a bird," I thought out loud.

After the laughter stopped, we resumed the hunt. Soon to my surprise and amazement Leukos pointed. We had lost him around the head of an old equipment lot when all of a sudden Paul exclaimed, "Look at that, Leukos is locked up." And sure enough he was, head and tail high, looking for all the world like a muddy statue of his father. Stone locked like a blue granite statue, he did not move until the birds were in the air and we were blasting away. And, of all things, Leukos retrieved a bird and chased down a cripple and fetched it in. Paul expressed his approval lavishly, while William only grunted and acknowledged that the dog had done his job. I began to feel that my dog was vindicating himself.

By and by Blue was nowhere to be found, and we suspected that she was on point somewhere. Having seen Leukos go around a fence row looking interested, I headed after him. "I'll check around here," I volunteered, walking briskly toward the fence row. Presently, I came upon the two. "Hey, you guys get over here, Leukos is locked up," I called.

My breathless friends quickly joined me expectantly. "He's locked up alright!" said Paul. "Locked in the throes of fornication!"

"Damn," William grunted, "I thought she went out of heat a week ago."

"Well, evidently Leukos didn't think so." Paul observed. "Sweet'n, looks like you are going to have some pretty drops."

III

House Dog

We had killed twenty-three birds, one less than the limit for us both. Paul and I were cleaning them over by the barn as William busied himself feeding his dogs. Leukos walked around stiff-legged and fatigued, finally settling on the door mat near the back steps after circling it several times. The night was warm for February, and there was a steady breeze from the south, confirming that the forecasted front was moving in. The air was heavy with the prospects of rain.

"Poolie, you finish these birds, and I'll take care of Leukos. You remember what happened last year when we got home," I said.

Paul grumbled his approval and agreed that it would be a good idea if I did just that. "You will no doubt be in deep trouble this year if you bring Leukos back to your child bride with him all matted with cockleburs like you did last year. Your besackus will be rawer than his was last year . . ." He was still muttering about my lack of attention to "Pretty Thing" as I moved out of earshot from him.

It was our second trip together to Early County to hunt with William. The first had been wonderful. Not only had we seen more birds than we usually did in a full season in Tallapoosa County, Alabama, but both of us had actually taken home a good mess of birds, despite the fact that, as William noted, we had not shot all the misses out of our guns before we came. Actually, the best thing about the first hunt was that William and I began a new and wonderful friendship that became the most compelling reason for the annual trips.

The day had begun just as it had the preceding year, with a cup of coffee at home and breakfast in Eufaula. As Paul said, we stopped for "BPs" (big pancakes) at the local "food emporium" (café) and were "at the ready." We picked up our three-day licenses just over the river in Georgetown and were soon sitting at William's round oak kitchen table. After a gusty greeting and handshakes, he let into Paul about women and sex and getting him "fixed up" for the night.

"Now, Paul. I know somebody who'll be happy to rub your back tonight so you will be ready to hunt again tomorrow." William winked at me, his blue eyes sparkling with the fun of the chase and hinting at the next jab. "And that ain't all she will rub, either."

"Sweet'n, you be nice." Paul was used to the assault and did not really seem to be bothered by it. It was a ritual that had been going on since college days. But occasionally he would glance at me as if wondering what I thought of the goings-on.

Paul had emptied the groceries that we had picked up at Fort Gains and was busy fixing ham sandwiches while William and I chatted at the table. "Doc, don't you think we ought to just drop ole Poolie off on the way back from the mullet house tonight? We could pick him up in the morning, and we could just bring his boots and his gun. Course it is likely that once this ole girl gets hold of him he won't be able to hunt. What ya say, Doc?" William had a way of trying to pull me into the attack.

"I think we should drop him off on our way to the mullet house," I said. "That way he won't be counting the beers we drink."

"Now, Doctor, y'all can give me all the grief you want, but why don't you just tell William about the hell you caught last year from Ruthie Mae when you brought Leukos home so matted up with cockleburs and sand spurs that he couldn't walk for a week." Paul began the counter attack.

William roared with laughter, "You took that petty thing back to momma all raw with cockleburs under his legs! Hell, Doc!"

"I did not realize that he was in such a bad shape until we got home," I confessed. "I cut so much hair off that dog that he looked more like a pointer than a setter. As a matter of fact, I gave him a trim job last night so maybe that won't be so much of a problem this year. By the way, William, how many drops did you get from the breeding last year?"

"None! I guess Leukos had not shot all the misses out of his gun, either. And if Paul will hurry up with the sandwiches, I'll let you boys miss some more birds."

Paul set the table, and we had grace. William thanked the Lord for the food and for our fellowship. He was sincere. I am sure that he relished our being there as much as we did.

Soon we were afield. It was an overcast day, and there was a soft westerly wind. William let us out of the Jeep at the "hog pen," and before we could load our guns the dogs pointed. William backed the Jeep to the dirt road where he could view the happenings. The dogs held rock solid. As we eased in front of the dogs, the birds burst from under our feet in a sudden, familiar roar of wings, decussating in a frantic unorganized escape. I shot twice at the right-most bird, knowing instinctively that I was well behind him. Paul missed also. We looked at each other and shook our heads. From the road William yelled, "How many did y'all get?"

He had seen the whole thing. There was almost laughter in his voice. "None."

"Damn. I thought sure that you would have shot all the misses out of those guns by this late in the season. Come on down the fence. Those birds all lit in the hedgerow between the road and the peanut field."

We exited over the hog wire fence topped with barbed wire all of it wrapped with honey suckle vine and half hidden like a booby trap. I fell twice in the attempt, realizing anew how important it is to unload before crossing fences and the like. Once over, we commenced to attack the hedge row. It was full of small cedars and sugarberry trees and various shrubs and all manner of leg-grabbing vines, some with briars. Paul got on the road side and I stayed on the field side of the tangle. Soon the action was intense. When we reached the end we had five birds and were feeling some better about the zero score on the covey rise.

William wanted to be debriefed about the covey and the number of points and how the dogs performed. He was also curious about why we had missed on the covey rise. "What is that you are shooting?"

"It is a Browning Lightning Twelve," I said.

"Ever considered getting a real bird gun, Doc?"

"Nothing wrong with the damn gun, William."

"Well, Doc, it's like this. I let you boys out at the hog pen and ole Leukos and Blue were pointed solid, and I know the birds got up right in front of you. I understand that Paul can't shoot because he's thinking about that ole girl I am going to fix him up with tonight, but Doc . . ." William's voice trailed off into other thoughts. "Hell, y'all load up the dogs, and let's go over across the road."

Perhaps now is a time to clear up a point about hunting with William. He never actually hunted with us; he acted as a guide. He drove us around in his brother's old M38 Jeep which had a dog box on the back and a place to ride two hunters on the top just behind the front seat. William drove, told us how to hunt an area and watched for the birds. His arthritis precluded his walking very much and would probably have kept him from being able to shoot a shotgun very well. We never really discussed this in detail, and occasionally he would put his gun up on the rack as if he intended to hunt also. He had hunted these fields since childhood and had killed his share of quail. He knew where the birds were likely to be and where they were likely to go when they flushed, and he had stories about previous hunts in every place we stopped. One thing was obvious: he wanted us to find birds and to have a good hunt. While he was not right with us every time we shot, he queried us when we got back to the Jeep and wanted us to account for every miss. It got to a point for me that I would just look William eyeball to eyeball and say, "Hell, William, I don't know why I missed that going away shot, but I for sure didn't do it on purpose. Guess I'm getting worse the older I get."

William would respond to my self-deprecation with, "Naw, Doc, I saw you drop those two on the rise over by the dry pond and drop that single through the thicket of the fence row."

"Yeah, but that was just luck," I would rejoin. "Even a blind hog can occasionally find an acorn."

Hunting in South Georgia is very different from what we were used to in the hills of east central Alabama. Back home we went to where we were going to hunt, let the dogs down and hunted, and when we were through, we put the dogs in the truck and went home—one stop hunting. At William's it was different, more like spot hunting. It didn't have to be that way, of course, but that was the way William did it. The real difference, however, was that there were a lot of quail in Early County, Georgia.

William took us across the highway to a part of the property that was passed down to his sister, Mamie. As he drove through an open gate, William stopped the Jeep. "Now, Paul," he said in almost a whisper. "I see those birds right now in that hedgerow. You and Doc get down and load up. I'll let ole Blue out when you are ready. One of you get on the other side, and both walk up the hedge row. The birds will get up before you get to that sugarberry tree."

We did as told. Blue slipped into the hedgerow and pointed. She was familiar with the scenario. She crept and stopped and moved up with us. Suddenly the birds flushed giving us both going-away shots as they skedaddled down the row. We both picked up birds. William let Leukos down, and we pressed in on the singles.

It looked like the birds flew about a hundred yards before pitching back into the hedge. Before we could get to them however, the dogs pointed a second covey. This covey behaved like the first. We both scored again. Soon we began getting up singles from the first covey. We followed the hedgerow and the one that cornered with it for nearly a mile, and we were constantly in birds. By the time we finished the round, the afternoon light was fading and the sky was becoming overcast. Paul had run out of ammunition, and I was loaning him shells, two at a time. We made one more stop on the way back to William's house, and we both managed to drop a bird each on the rise of the covey we found only a few feet from where we parked the Jeep. This was more birds than we had ever killed together in the forty plus years that we had been hunting.

Back at Williams, Paul finished cleaning the birds, and I took care of Leukos who had done himself proud that day. I think even William was impressed with his pointing and retrieving. I fed him well and clipped a few cockleburs from behind his ears while I whispered how proud I was of him and loved on him. Fortunately the trim job I had given him the night before was very effective in preventing the severe matting that had occurred the year earlier. Just as we finished our chores, it began to rain softly.

I had planned to feed him and put him in the dog box for the night. The first visit he had whined and howled when I chained him to a tree next to his box. Feeling sorry for him and knowing he would not go off during the night, I turned him lose and left him outside. He settled back down on the mat at the foot of the back steps and went to sleep immediately. I watched him for a long moment reminiscing about what had happened the first year. It was a deep embarrassment to me. Leukos was to me a friend and companion, but to Ruth he was a childlike pet whom she pampered and hand fed and let sleep on the kitchen floor under the table.

I can honestly blame my sweet wife for indirectly causing the problem that night. The first inkling I had that she and I had different ideas about the care and feeding of bird dogs was in 1987. We had built our dream house on the farm at the edge of town, and I had a fence company build a large dog pen with a six-foot high chain link fence. It was nice and enclosed more than an acre. I had a galvanized tin dog house for my then dog, Jed. Things went well for a day or so, but when I got home from work each evening, Jed would be out of the pen. I would always put him back again and search for his escape spot, which I never found. Not being totally naive, I soon realized that Ruth was letting him out as soon as I went to work every day. When confronted with my clever deductions, she admitted that she had done so because he was "unhappy being locked in the pen." And so it was that every day she let him out and every evening I put him back. This continued until Jed would no longer come when I called. As a matter of fact, he avoided me totally. After coming to terms with the reality that I had lost that battle, I just left the gate open so he could come and go as he chose. He chose to never go back into the pen, and soon we became friends again.

It was not long before Ruth decided that Jed could come into the house occasionally as long as he did not get off the tile in the kitchen and breakfast room. She let him sleep in the house when it was really cold, or when it was really hot. And it pleased him to be in the house a lot of the time; seems like he always needed to cool off in the summer and get warm in the winter.

When I got Leukos, I knew that the pen was not an option because, "You are not going to put that puppy in the dog pen. He will be lonely and he will wonder why Jed gets to come in the house and he can't." When I suggested that he would not get so lonely if Jed were to be in the pen, too, she said something to the effect that "if you are going to have a dog, Buster, you are going to treat him right." I gave up.

It so happened that on the first hunt down at William's even after I let Leukos off the chain he howled. I finally put him in the dog box and moved him to the far corner of the yard hoping that his singing would not keep everyone awake. It didn't keep me awake because I was dead tired from the walking. I woke a couple of times in the night as is my custom since prostate surgery, and each time he was howling the most pitiful pleas imaginable. The coyotes not too far away joined in the hymn at times. I went to his box just to be sure he was ok and that he had enough water. All seemed well except he was unhappy. I think he missed Momma, and I was glad that she was not there to witness his misery.

The next morning we had found a couple of coveys and were up-loading the dogs in the Jeep when William made a remark that let me know that his sleep had been disturbed by the rudeness of my dog and that perhaps we should make some other arrangements tonight.

After the afternoon hunt, it was clear that Leukos was tired, really tired. He lay under the carport near the back door steps and slept as we ate supper. He had been fed and watered, and he welcomed some steak scraps only if handed to him so he wouldn't have to get up.

"Ole Pretty Thing is one tired dog, Doc." William observed. "Why don't you just leave him right here tonight? He's not going anywhere, and maybe he won't sing outside the box."

I agreed that it was a good idea, and when we went to bed Leukos was still asleep in the carport. I slept well that night. The only howling sounds were from the coyotes harmonizing in the distance.

I was jolted from sleep by Paul's call of reveille. At lease that was what I thought at first. He sounded like a hard core Marine drill sergeant trying to awaken his troops. "Good God, Leukos! What are you doing in the house?"

There he was, sleeping on a throw-rug near the foot of the bed. Unaccustomed as he was to such a rude awakening, Leukos rolled over on his back and lay motionless. "Out you go, you sorry beast, or off goes your head and a big chunk of your ass!" Paul had a way with words. I made my way to the bedroom door, and we glanced at each other. "Out! Out! William will never invite us back, Doc, if you let your sorry hound sleep in the house."

"I didn't let him in," I protested sleepily.

"Well, it's for sure that I didn't," he muttered as he dragged the still supine dog across the hard wood floor and out the front door which was standing open. "Here's how he got in. Some damn fool left the front door open!"

"William never locks the door, you know," I whispered. "Leukos must have pushed the door open like he does at home."

At breakfast I profusely apologized to William and explained what had happened. "I'm afraid my bride has taught my dogs all sorts of bad habits," I finally said, passing the buck.

"Don't worry about it, Doc," he said with a wink. "There have been worse things than that sleeping in that room. Matter of fact, Paul, that ole girl that I'm going to invite over to entertain you tonight slept right there. Hell, Sweet'n, you yell at her like you did poor ole Leukos and she will roll over on her back just like he did."

"Be nice," Paul said.

We finished our steaks and potatoes, and the salad Paul made. William and I washed ours down with cold beer and Paul with iced tea. Paul was washing the dishes while William and I sat at the ancient oak table, talking farming and politics and were having some "brown water" for an after dinner attitude adjustment. We were mellow. What a day!

It was beginning to rain a soft, cool February rain. The sleep monster was working on me. It had already taken Leukos to the balmy land of somnambulant bliss. But I began to reflect on last year and Leukos coming in the house, and said that I suppose I ought to take Leukos and his box to the old barn and bed him down for the night.

"Hell, Doc, the sombich can sleep with Paul tonight." William was drawing deep at the amber liquid.

"The hell you say!"

"Think I'll just put him in the barn. That way, if he hollows, he won't bother us. He seems really tired and will probably sleep all night. Looks like the rain has set in." I slipped on my boots and took the reluctant dog to the barn and shut him in his dog box. I sloshed back to the house in a trot and took off my boots at the back steps. It was going to be a rainy night.

It did rain. The heavens opened and down it came. It was a frog choker, a gulley washer, a turd floater. As they used to say down at the Climax Café, it was raining like a cow pissing on a flat rock. I watched the silver streaks against the yard light until the sleep monster carried me away. Come morning, it was still raining. Water stood in pools in the yard. There would be no more hunting this weekend.

William and I were sitting at the table drinking coffee and telling jokes while Paul was frying eggs and bacon. "How 'bout ole "Pretty Thing?" asked William.

"He's in the barn in his box," I said after a long draw of hot coffee.

"Which barn, Doc?"

"The old one, the one with that old truck half buried in the mud," said I.

"Doc, that barn is at least a foot below grade. Leukos is up to his ass in water! That is if he hasn't floated down to the river."

"Oh, hell!" I muttered as I grabbed my boots from the back steps and ran to the barn through the rain.

At first I did not see him. The inside of the barn looked like a swimming pool. I was horrified. Finally several feet from where I had placed his box the night before, I espied him. He was shivering and up to his knees in water and not happy. As I opened the cage, he dashed to the car port where he lay on the mat and began licking the water and mud off himself. Initially the water had floated him, almost washing his ark out of the barn, but as he moved about the water came in swamping it to the bottom.

"Leukos alright?" inquired Paul as I closed the kitchen door.

"Just pissed off."

"Yeah. He is not the only one who will be when she finds out what happened to her Pretty Thing. Doc, you are going to be in deep trouble again."

I didn't tell Ruth, not for a couple of years. I was telling her some William stories and somehow incidentally injected it in the yarn.

"Sometimes I think that for you to be a doctor you're not very smart," she said shaking her head.

IV

Men and Birds

The dogs were pointed, Leukos and Blue directly in front of us demanding our attention to a clump of high weeds and briars not twenty yards from the fence corner, and Liz was holding steady at a 45 degree angle to their right. It was picture perfect, so classic that you could not tell who had pointed first and who was backing. Leukos was standing head high, tail sweeping up in a slight arch with the very tip pointing forward, the hair feathering down like the plume on a drum major's hat, and in the sunlight of a clear February afternoon he was whiter than white. The two pointers crouched stiff and motionless, except for the almost unperceivable tremor of their tails.

Paul and I hurried across the field toward the trio of dogs, he left and I right, as William watched from the Jeep on the near side of the field. When we got to about twenty feet of the clump of tall brown grass interlaced with swirls and tangles of briar, we stopped briefly to catch our breaths. I wiped my sweaty right hand across my shirt and felt my heart pounding, pounding like it always did when I approached pointed dogs. God! Some things don't change. The thrill, the anticipation, the tremor in my hands, the pounding in my chest—just like it was the first time I approached pointed dogs with my dad forty-five years earlier.

I glanced at Paul. He nodded and said almost in a whisper, "Ok."

"Let's ease up," I said, taking a nervous, tentative step forward. Soon I was even with Blue, still frozen on point. I slid my thumb to the base of the safety and could feel it trembling against the corrugations. Without turning my head, I could see Paul in my peripheral vision, his orange cap and vest blazing in the sun. I wondered briefly if his mouth was dry, and if he felt his heart pound, if his hands were wet or trembling at all.

Suddenly as if hearing a silent 'charge,' the dogs bounded toward some invisible target, and just as suddenly there was—nothing. Nothing! No covey rise. Not even a rabbit. With tails flailing like sweepers and noses snorting aromas near the ground the dogs endeavored to nose birds out of the empty patch.

"What!" Paul sounded almost relieved.

"I thought sure that they had . . ." I began, only to be interrupted by the abrupt tumult of flailing wing beats as the frantic birds rose ten feet to my right.

The dry mouth and the pounding heart were unnoticed. There was no anticipatory trembling, no sweaty hands. Everything became automatic, just instinct formed from unremembered recollections of hundreds of previous covey rises. Some reflex thumbed the safety, shouldered the Superposed, pointing it at the bird some autopilot had selected, and tugged the trigger. The reassuring pop of the gun and the pressure at my shoulder were ignored as I watched the tumbling bird and the trailing billow of feathers. It was a touch down, a home run; it was a victory, the game was over! I did not shoot the top barrel, but pulled on the safety and watched the birds sail across the fence into scattered small pine and sedge.

"Birds were playing hide and seek with you, Doc?" William asked as he drove up in the Jeep. "Didn't hear you shoot but once. What are you trying to do, save your bullets?"

"Why press my luck?" I responded. "Why spoil a perfect game? The dogs pointed and held. I killed the first bird I shot at, and the dog retrieved it. Hell, that is perfect, William, perfect! That is what bird hunting is all about: the dog, the bird and the bird hunter. What more do you want?"

"I want you to get the limit, Doc. The limit set forth by the Georgia Wildlife Commission is twelve, not one. Hell, don't you appreciate a good covey rise?"

"I got my two, Sweet'n," Paul joined in, "but that probably won't happen again for a couple of years. I say we go look for some singles and stop jabbering about not shooting twice. He'd have just missed anyway, most likely."

"Thanks for the expression of confidence," I said as I slid a shell in the bottom chamber. "Let's hunt the singles."

It was my third trip to Early County with Paul to hunt with William. We had arrived at noon Georgia time and had eaten sandwiches and pound cake, the latter a contribution from one of William's lady-friends, and all of it properly blessed by Paul. Sitting around the old oak kitchen table we downed several glasses of iced tea while engaged in conversation that did not lend itself to termination, and we lingered in heavy discussion, recollection and speculation until well past two o'clock. Paul hinted that we might want to go afield when William suddenly brightened, his blue eyes twinkling with delight, "Now, Paul, the Doc and I can drop you off down at Blakely and hunt the Harris place and pick you up at dark. There is this ole girl who can make you glad you didn't go hunting. What ya say, Sweet'n?"

"Be nice. Be nice, William."

"Hell, I'm being nice, Paul. I'm just giving you an option."

"I bet the dogs are ready to go hunting," I interrupted. "First thing you know we are going to waste the whole afternoon bumping our gums. Besides that, we've got to wait for Paul to lather up with all that sunscreen."

"And Paul," William said, obviously delighted that he had an additional topic to kid Paul about, "why do you have to put on something that smells like an Hawaiian fruit drink?"

"Well, I just do, Sweet'n. I just do, so you might as well get used to it."

"Trouble is, Paul, that it makes me want to drink rum and lie in the sun."

"You can certainly do it, William. There's not a cloud in the sky," Paul retorted as he grabbed his gun and vest and headed for the Jeep.

It was a bird hunting day in South Georgia! The sky was robin egg blue and totally clear. A light breeze now and then seemed to come from no particular direction, and the temperature mid afternoon was fifty-five. Sunshine on a single shirt and hunting vest felt good. We both had enough forethought to bring a jacket for the ride in the Jeep, which I enjoyed from atop the dog box while Paul manned the passenger seat beside William. I did not catch a lot of the conversation between the two, but I could tell that William was still in the attack mode for I could hear him begin, "Now, Paul . . ." And I could hear Paul saying from time to time, "Now be nice, William, be kind to the Poolie." And I could hear William laughing.

We hunted the singles from the first covey and were fortunate enough to collect a couple more birds. The next stop was at the "old warehouse field" across the corner from William's house. It was productive also as was the next stop around an old cotton field which had been fallow for three years and had recently been converted to pine. Paul and I were both shooting pretty well, we thought. William disagreed, of course. He wanted an explanation for all our misses.

The afternoon began to take on the shades of evening, and I began to feel cool. The ride back to the house was no fun at all. The thirty mile an hour wind chill on top of the Jeep was pure torture, especially in a shirt still damp from sweating and a right pant leg wet from a step into a hidden drain ditch. Paul and William were at least partially out of the wind behind the windshield. My hands were so stiff when we got back that I was little help to Paul cleaning the birds, but somehow we managed it.

William penned his dogs and fed them while I fed Leukos, who had already bedded down on the mat beside the back door. By then Paul was at the kitchen sink still picking meticulously at the days kill and complaining about my lack of assistance. I explained that I was cold, too cold to do anything except take a hot shower, and proceeded to do just that. Once toasty warm and dry inside a sweater and lined chinos, I slipped on wool socks and slippers and joined the two sitting in the carport before the flaming grill. The old Mercury Cougar gave us protection from most of the night breeze.

My arrival had interrupted a new onslaught about the wild women of Early County whom William could arrange for Paul to stay with tomorrow while we hunted. I changed the subject, "William, I was poking about while Poolie was cleaning the birds awhile ago, and went to inspect your barn. That turkey gobbler you've got back there in a coupe got to flapping when I walked by and nearly made me mess up my pants! What the heck is that all about?"

"Well, Doc . . . ." There was a long pause as William's mouth widened. "You just met Ollie."

"You fattening him up for Easter?"

William laughed long and hard until the laugh became a cough. By and by he stopped coughing. "Doc, turkey season comes in on March the first, and Ollie and I are going turkey hunting. He is my best turkey hunting partner."

"Naw!"

"Doc, you don't take a gobbler hunting with you?"

"I think you are blowing smoke up my ass."

"There is nothing that brings in an old gobbler like another gobbler. I just tie Ole Ollie out there beside that hen decoy over there on the steps," he said nodding at a rubber hen decoy half hidden in a cardboard box filled with boots and tackle boxes and unopened cartons of tractor parts.

"Isn't it against the law to hunt turkeys with decoys?" I ventured.

"Not in Georgia."

"How about a *live* decoy?" Paul was more incensed than inquisitive.

"Now Paul, that's what we need for you: a live decoy! I could fix you up for sure!"

We ate steak, talked politics and farming, and told a few jokes. We even ventured into religion briefly and superficially, concluding finally and absolutely that God is good. Paul washed dishes. Meanwhile William and I poured some brown water and sipped at the amber liquid that warms the heart and loosens the tongue, and the evening and night completed the first day.

Morning came early it seemed. Paul banged on my door hollering, "Reveille! Reveille!" sounding like some gung ho Marine drill sergeant, each word grading on the softness of sleep. I slipped on my dry boots, pulled a jacket over my pajamas and slouched into the kitchen grabbing a cup of coffee before settling at the table across from William. We sipped coffee and exchanged groans as Paul began frying bacon.

"I slept like a stone," I said clearing my throat with a draw of hot coffee, "but was rudely awakened by some jar-head beating on the door and yelling."

"Yeah, well you probably weren't disturbed by some decoy gobbling before the sun came up like I was. Dang, William, looks like you would have told Ollie that you have company."

"Paul, if you were as pure in heart as the Doc and I, you'd have slept right through the gobbling just like we did. Besides, Ollie is practicing up; he wants to be in good voice come opening day. You know, he doesn't get to sit in on choir practice."

"Oh, hell, no." Paul said in a voice just under a scream, "The damn turkey can't hold cards in his feet."

"Yeah, but, Paul some of the choir members can."

The morning had happened clear and crisp. A light frost was still present on the shaded areas as we loaded the Jeep. As I slid his electronic collar on and loaded Leukos, I could hear the beginning of a new attack. "Now Paul, the Doc and I can just drop you off . . ."

"Paul, it's your turn to ride on top," I interrupted, "I'm still cold from the ride home yesterday."

I settled in the seat next to William, and we were off. "Now, Doc," he began and I realized that it was my turn to take flack from William. "Why is it that you need to put that Alabama Power Company on ole Leukos? You need to jump start him every now and then?"

"No," I said. Then after a long pause. "But he used to be hard of hearing."

"Fixed that?"

"Yeah."

As luck would have it, we got into a covey of birds almost as soon as we let the dogs down. Blue was the first to point; and as Paul and I approached, the other two dogs came up from our left and honored her. The old pointers were crouched, shoulders low and hind quarters high; Leukos was standing tall and stiff, head high as if trying to see over as many obstacles as possible. I wished I had remembered to bring a camera.

The birds flushed to the left in Paul's direction, all except one that zigzagged through the limbs of a small water oak and bore right. My first shot brought down some twigs and left over leaves, and the second shot went into the wild blue yonder several feet behind the frantic bird. I knew the instant I squeezed the trigger that I had missed. Fortunately, Paul had downed one bird which Blue retrieved. William demanded an explanation for the misses, and all I could say was that I just couldn't catch up with the bird.

We found some singles along the fence row next to a freshly disked cotton field and were lucky enough to increase our bag. One bird flew out across the field, and I dropped it on the second shot. Only crippled, the bird began to run across the soft ground with me in hot pursuit all along calling for Leukos, who did not appear particularly interested in the foot race. We had run probably fifty yard when I realized that the ground was wet and soft and that I was having trouble lifting my feet. The mud stuck to my boots like soft glue making ever increasing clods. Fatigue forced me to stop half way across as I watched the bird disappear into the opposite fence row. As I pondered my fate, I heard distant laughter and saw William leaning over the hood of the Jeep, slapping it as if it were some old drinking buddy, and I could see the three reluctant dogs sitting next to the Jeep as if enjoying the show. Finally, William yelled that they would meet me on the other side of the field, "Just keep going, Doc."

Never have my legs been so tired. I stopped several times hoping to find a place to sit down or even drop to a knee, but I was in a low area of the field and water from last week's rain had pooled there, and the new plowed ground was a gummy unpleasant glop. Slowly I lugged to my waiting companions who had retrieved the bird and were talking loudly about the exhibition they had just witnessed.

"The bird was faster than you on foot, Doc."

"Shut up!" I growled, sitting on the ground trying to scrape the mud off my boots. "I thought I had gotten into quick sand."

"Water runs down hill, Doc John," Paul chimed in, "and these fields just look flat."

"I'm too damn old to be doing this! What the hell was I thinking?"

"Even ole Leukos knew better than to get out in that field." William's face was red from laughing. "Or maybe he's gotten hard of hearing again."

"I wish I had that collar on you!" Tossing my cap in the Jeep, I lay back on the ground and ran my fingers through sweat soaked hair. "When I'm able to get up, I'm riding on top."

V

Toby

I remember well the first time I met Toby. It was our fourth trip to William's and we had just finished our sandwiches. He rolled into the back yard in a cloud of dust piloting a new Chevrolet super cab truck. A yellow lab was standing on the tool box.

Toby slid out of the truck showing a wide smile, wearing blue jeans and a camouflage jacket. Judging from my boys, I figured him to be in his late twenties. As he approached with the swagger of a work horse, long plodding steps, his hand extended as if he were running for sheriff.

"Let's go hunting," said William. "If last year was any indication, these boys are going to need all the help they can get." Then he introduced us.

"Come on," insisted William. "Let's go hunting."

"I have already been hunting," Toby replied. "Look in the back of my truck and you'll see." We followed him to his truck. "This is my lab, Denver," he said, nodding to the dog sitting on his tool box keeping guard over the game in the bed of the truck, and looking proud.

There was a rabbit, several doves and two quail. "I got these on the way over here from my house." This would have impressed me even more had I known that Toby lived less than a mile down the dirt road (just take a right at the cross roads there at William's).

Then with a look of I-wish-I-could, Toby said, "I promised my wife that I would pick up Bailey at school and take her to her granddad's house. Maybe I can catch up with y'all tomorrow afternoon. I'll bring the Mule." Soon he was off in a cloud of red Georgia dust, Denver looking for all the world like a stage coach driver in a Roy Rogers movie.

As Paul would say, the afternoon hunt was a "non-event." We found some birds that mostly got up wild. We missed a few "give-me" shots, and we even walked up a couple of coveys of birds. We both had briar scratches all over and were hot and tired. The one bird that Paul had managed to drop had been chewed pretty well by Leukos, and Paul was complaining bitterly and loudly. "Damn dog thinks I walked through all those briars and shot this bird for him. And he didn't even point it! This will definitely be the Doc's bird if we kill enough to take home. Leukos has softened it up mighty well . . ."

We had the traditional steak, potatoes, salad and bread, washed down by large glasses of iced tea, all of course preceded by a blessing, or as we say in the South, by "Grace." William thanked the Father for the food, the fellowship and all our many blessings. They pray in South Georgia the same way we do in Central Alabama. Once done eating, we cleared the table, and Paul commenced to wash the dishes. Meanwhile, William and I poured ourselves a "refreshing beverage" and settled down at the old oak table to philosophize about various things, and to catch up on what had happened since the last year's hunt.

I noticed two decks of cards and some poker chips on the counter next to the table. "Looks like you had 'choir practice' recently, William."

"Thursday night, Doc. And I suspect that is the reason Toby did not hunt with us may have had something to do with choir practice."

"Good Gosh! William," Paul joined in. "Surely you are not corrupting the youth of Early County!"

"Toby was pretty much corrupted before he joined the choir. It was more like an education he got Thursday. Problem was he stayed up too late, or something. I think he must have gotten in trouble when he got home, but he would never admit it."

"Tell us about Toby," said I. "I get the impression he must be quite the hunter."

"Hell, Doc, you'll just have to see for yourself. Toby . . ." William gazed out the window and never finished the sentence. There was a long silence, just Paul splashing dish water and humming to himself.

"Doc," William said after a long draught of amber relaxation, "you're looking good; are you having any more trouble with that prostate cancer?"

"Not with the cancer, not just now. Just with a lab test. The PSA is creeping up ever so slowly. But it's not a problem, and I feel good. Matter of fact, one more brown water and I'll feel real damn good." We both laughed, but I could tell that he was concerned that there was a test that was not good. I changed the subject. We knocked back another drink and ended the evening telling jokes, relating stories and talking bird dog. We even heard the real account of what happened at choir practice.

I had showered while William and Paul cooked the steaks, so I was ready for bed instantly. I fell into the old double bed, pulled up the down comforter, mumbled a word of gratitude to the Maker, and was immediately asleep. After a couple of hours I awoke hot and sweating under the insulation of the down comforter, so I slipped out through the open front door and into the yard.

It was a beautiful night. The stars were everywhere in the sky, the rim of a new moon barely visible above the tree line. "What a day!" I thought. "What a time to be alive." The world seemed peaceful, and all seemed right. It was a moment I wanted to hold on to and relive over and over. Then suddenly there was the recollection of the cancer thing, but I pushed it back out of mind with the thought that I would worry about it when I had to, not tonight. Not in South Georgia, not with my friends.

I noticed that Leukos was asleep just outside the front door on the porch mat. He didn't move as I passed. For some reason he had decided not to come in the house. I smiled at him and said, "Momma'd be proud." I crawled back in bed and thought about Ruth till I went to sleep.

I opened my eyes and lay still. I could hear the clutter in the kitchen and the muffled voices of Paul and William busying around fixing breakfast, pretending to fuss at each other. The bed felt good; it was hard to move. Finally slipping from the covers, I was welcomed by a dull aching hurt in my low back. Always the first thought, always, the health issue. Could this be a symptom? I tried not to dwell on it; after all, I thought, I am approaching sixty. Hell, I ought to hurt, especially after all the walking we did yesterday. I pulled on my hunting pants and a shirt and joined my friends in the kitchen.

"Well, Doctor, welcome to the world of the living." Paul was frying bacon. William was sitting at the old table drinking coffee. "Pour yourself a cup and sit there with Sweet'n, and I'll have breakfast in a second."

William was sipping coffee, both hands around the cup, gnarled fingers interlaced. I am sure the heat felt good to his arthritic fingers. He was chucking to himself. "Morning, Doc. I was just trying to decide if we ought to let Paul off down the road where this ole girl lives that I was telling you about. Hell, he ain't going to kill any birds, not the way he was shooting yesterday. We could just pick him up on our way back from the mullet house. That way he would be rested up to cook breakfast again tomorrow. What do you think?"

"I can't make decisions before I have at least one cup of coffee," I said, sitting down beside him.

"Doc, you have to make all sorts of decisions, twenty-four hours a day. What do you mean you got to have coffee first? You make decisions at two o'clock in the morning without coffee, don't you?" William was getting cranked up.

"No. Not big decisions, like about Poolie and bird hunting. I am leaving that decision up to the two of you."

"But you're a doctor," continued William.

"William, you won't believe this, but Ruthie Mae puts out the clothes he is to wear every day. Hell, he can't even decide on the color of his tie!" Paul was obviously trying to get the discussion away from himself.

"That true, Doc?"

"Yes, but that has nothing to do with making decisions," said I.

"What the hell does it have to do with then?" William was bent over laughing; laughing loud staccato laughs that gradually became loud staccato coughs.

"Well, it seems that she never liked what I picked out, and she would always insist that I changed ties or shirts or something. Said that I didn't match. I finally got tired of changing clothes two or three times each morning, and told her, 'Why don't you just get out what you want me to wear. It would sure simplify things.' She has been getting my clothes out ever since. She says I'm a tacky dresser, and the way I dress is a reflection on her—makes her look like she's not taking good care of me."

William exploded in laughter that again trailed off into a deep rattling cough. I could tell that he was once a heavy smoker.

Before long we were loaded up in my truck, William driving, his brother having taken the Jeep back to Albany. William's truck didn't run most of the time, least that is what he said.

We found some birds in an overgrown field next to an old cotton-holding barn. The dogs worked them well, but the birds got up in wild confusion right at the edge of the woods and immediately made their escape, except for two. Leukos retrieved them both, unchewed.

William advised that we go on through the woods and he would meet us at the power line. We did as told. On two or three occasions we heard singles getting up, but neither of us got a shot. When we got to the power line, Leukos was on point. We eased up beside him, Paul on right and I on left. We passed Leukos and nothing happened, not for a few more steps. Then as if propelled by a rocket, a bob shot from between us 180 degrees from the way we were facing, spewing a white stream as it jettisoned the contents of its cloaca and barely clearing the perplexed dog. I shot twice out of respect for the supersonic fowl, so did Paul.

"Good Gosh!" screamed Paul. "That is the fastest bird I have ever seen! He had afterburners!"

"Yes, I saw him drop them about the time he cleared Leukos," I agreed. "That is clearly an example of the expression 'a-shittin'-and a-gettin'.'"

"And he was doing that!"

We told William all about the rocket propelled quail over a sandwich and beer—or in Paul's case, a Coke at noon. "Early County birds are fast alright," he laughed.

It was high noon Georgia time when Toby puttered up in a Kawasaki Mule. "Ya'll about ready?" he yelled from the back door. We were still sitting at the kitchen table. "Would have been here earlier," he said as he plopped down across from William, "but I had to stop by Saxton's and pick up a six-pack."

"Good," approved William. "It's going to be hot this afternoon."

"Maybe I should have gotten two six-packs."

"Naw," I said, "Poolie doesn't drink beer, and I don't either, not till after the guns have been put away."

"I know," laughed Toby, "I was thinking about for William and me. Hell, we're going to get hot just watching you and Mr. Paul bust briars!"

William was nodding, rocking back and forward, his face red with the conflict of a belly laugh and a spasm of coughing. "Paul would shoot better if he had a beer or two. Hell, he couldn't do any worse. Course, we could just drop him off over at that old gal's and leave a six-pack. What do you say, Sweet'n?"

"Let's go hunting," said Paul, anticipating the usual harangue.

We talked a few more minutes and soon learned that Toby was twenty-nine years old, that he had two children, a daughter Bailey, who was nearly four and a son, Alex, just a few months old. His wife, Brandi, taught first grade. She and Toby, both from the Blakely area, lived less than a mile from William near the next cross road to the east.

Toby had gone to college at Auburn and was very familiar with the Alex City area, especially Lake Martin, where he had fished a lot while in school. He was a forestry graduate, as was his dad and older brother, Woody. His dad, who worked many years for Georgia Pacific, had helped the boys get set up in the timber producing business. They had worked hard and, early on, had become very successful. Things were good for Toby.

He also inquired as to what we did. "So," he said almost as if drawing a conclusion, "Mr. Paul is a retired Marine Major, and you are a cancer doctor. Damn!"

"That's about it," I confirmed, not knowing which fact was responsible for the expletive. "Let's go hunting. I guess Leukos will load in that fancy rig of yours."

The Mule was fixed with the most beautiful elevated seat and dog box I have ever seen. His dad, whose hobby is wood crafting, had made it using some sort of exotic wood imported from South America. It was high enough so that the riders could hold to the back of the ROPS and could look over the top of the mule. There was a compartment for guns and ammunition and a place to keep an extra jacket or vest or whatever. There were two dog compartments, each fitted with a water bucket, and there was a rack on the back for water. Nice rig!

We stopped at a couple of places and hunted without finding birds. By two o'clock Paul and I were nearly exhausted. As we completed the next round and neared the Mule, we observed William and Toby in deep conversation, each sipping a beer. As we approached, they both commented on how it was really hot and getting more humid. Paul and I agreed reaching for a Coke. "Why don't we go some place where we can find some birds," grumbled Paul.

We did stop another mile down the dirt road. The breeze at the top of the box blowing through our sweaty shirts felt really good. As we got down, William said matter-of-factly, "There ought to be a covey of birds right there where those two fences join. One of you ought to cross right here where the fence is down and the other hunt on this side."

Paul crossed the fence. There I was in full view of Heckle and Jeckle, knowing the critique I would get should there be birds as William predicted. The birds were there. The dogs pointed. As we walked up slowly, I could hear William mumbling in the back ground. The birds bolted up in mass confusion flying in every direction, some left at the corner, some across the field, and some back down the fence we had just walked up. I picked out the first bird I saw, but he banked around toward Paul. I turned on the next bird that made a sharp circle to my right. Swinging, I could see Toby scrunching down in the Mule, so I checked the swing. Then I glimpsed a late bird that seemed as confused as I. I swung the barrel just past him and fired what I thought would be an easy kill. But it didn't fall. I touched off the upper barrel with equal confidence, knowing I had an audience. It didn't fall. But it cut sharply in a wide circle sixty or so feet from the Mule. I watched in amazement as the bird crumpled in a shower of feathers as Toby zipped his gun from the rack under the seat and fired one shot. "Damn, damn, damn!" I muttered under my breath. "How in the world could that have happened?" William was roaring with delight.

So the afternoon went. So my confidence went. I don't remember killing any birds after that. There was a lot of commentary about my shooting, and, thank God, that I didn't shoot them.

By the time we returned to William's house, the sky was overcast and the humidity was high. My clothes were wet from sweat, mostly. Paul and I were exhausted as were the dogs. Toby disappeared in a roar.

We did our chores, showered and changed into jeans. William and I had a brown water while we awaited Toby's return. William choked several times while he told Paul over and over about the splendid display of bird shooting he had witnessed. He wheezed and laughed and coughed, his face red and tears running down his cheeks. Every time he described a scene, he would finish up with, "Damn! Doc!" And so it went until Toby returned all clean and slicked down. Then he repeated the story from his perspective, to the delight of William who was so contorted with laughter that he could hardly breathe.

"And I thought Doc was going to shoot my ass," Toby reported, "but he pulled up."

"I should have," was all I could mutter.

Soon we were headed to down town Blakely in William's Cougar. It coughed and sputtered pretty much like William, but I was surprised the old Mercury cranked. The road was steamy with fog and the night air was heavy and wet when we arrived at the mullet house. I can't remember what the real name of the café was, and it is not important. The food was good; I especially loved the mullet and flounder. Come to find out, Toby's uncle ran the place and did the cooking. We ate a lot of fried fish, onion rings and hushpuppies. We drank gallons of tea. William and Toby had conversations with dozens of people. It seemed they both knew the whole world. By and by we decided to head home.

The fog was increasing. It reminded me of the dust from William's road after a car passed. The Cougars' head lights penetrated about fifty yards, and William eased along cautiously. I could hardly keep my eyes open. I was full, exhausted, and sleepy. There wasn't much conversation, not even from Toby. Occasionally William would snicker, and Toby would echo.

I don't know where we were, somewhere outside of Blakely, somewhere on a paved road. Puttering through the dense fog it seemed like it was taking forever to get back. Suddenly there was a soft "Puff," a muffled explosion, and everything went white. Steam filled the Cougar.

"Get out! Get out!" screamed Toby. "We're on fire! We're going to burn up. Get out!"

We weren't going fast and William stopped the car almost immediately. I recall two distinct sounds from that moment; one was Toby's loud breathing and his clamoring to find the door handle; the other was William's laughter trailing into a spasm of coughing. We exited the Cougar, steam blowing from the hood and the inside of the car. Toby appeared to be in shock. "We ain't on fire, Toby," William said, "just blew a hose."

"I thought sure we were on fire. Scared hell out of me," Toby admitted, his voice quivering and his breath short as he paced up and down the road. "I couldn't see a thing, and couldn't find the door handle."

"You sure sounded like it, screaming and hollering and flailing around trying to get out. You better shake your britches."

Paul had not said much, but muttered matter-of-factly, "The Cougar just died."

VI

Dawson's Dog

Dawson Holman was barely nineteen when he joined the Navy on December 8, 1941, the day after the Japanese attack on Pearl Harbor, and he did not return home until four years later. Dawson was tall, rugged, good looking and loquacious—a lad who knew no stranger. After the war he built a successful floor finishing business, and like many of his rural Deep South peers, he farmed on the side. The tradition of dogs and bird hunting was as much a part of his up bringing as was civility and honor. When the town's men gathered for coffee at the Climax Café and the subject of quail hunting came up, Dawson's name was invariably mentioned. Though he's getting long in the tooth now, in his prime he was a whiz bang bird hunter. During the season he hunted four or five days a week, but it was his dog training that made him a legend, that and his genuine enthusiasm for bird hunting. He always had good dogs. It was generally acknowledged that his were as good if not better than any in the county, except remotely those of Booger Adams or Ily Taunton. He was a hard hunter, a fast walker, unstoppable by briar or branch, and he expected the same of his dogs, hunting them hard.

As the years went by, Dawson retired from "real" work but remained active and continued to hunt even as the quail population in Central Alabama began to dramatically decline. As patch farming virtually vanished and the big timber companies owned more and more of the old hunting areas, planting them in loblolly pine, quail hunting became almost impossible in our area. Because of his reputation, or perhaps karma, he was asked to guide at various quail plantations. Clients liked to hunt with him because of his fine dogs and, of course, his charming conversation and genteel manner. And he loved the opportunity to hunt every day, even if it wasn't really bird hunting. Most of all, Dawson Holman was a fine man, a gentleman.

I enjoyed talking to Dawson. He never lacked for a story or two, and he told them with unsuppressed gusto. One day in November he came for an office visit. After finishing with the medical matters, we drifted into a conversation about bird hunting. Initially, we lamented the decline of the quail population in Central Alabama, then somehow the desultory conversation migrated to South Georgia and the annual trip Paul and I made to Early County. By and by, Dawson began to inquire about my dogs, which was as natural as an old friend asking about my children or my wife. I told him about Leukos and mentioned that he was getting some age on and was not able to hunt three days in a row.

"Doc," he said, "why don't you take ole Rock with you this year? I think that he is the best dog I've ever had. He will do it all." Dawson was ebullient, his voice nearly pleading.

"I don't know. That is a big responsibility. I'd hate to think that if . . ."

"Doc, I trust you with my health, with my life. You know I'd trust you with my dog. It's no big deal. I would like for you to hunt with a really good dog."

I began to crawfish, not being high on borrowing another man's dog. It was too much like borrowing a child. Dawson, the quintessential salesman, persisted. I was finally able to put him off with, "Well, I'll think about it," figuring that I could find a way to gracefully tell him "no" by February.

I chanced to mention the encounter to Ruth that night. It was more like thinking out loud, but before I realized it I had rehashed our entire conversation. "Don't even think about it!" she said as if talking to one of the children about going to a suspect party. "You don't need to borrow anyone's dog, especially not to take to South Georgia, and especially for a weekend. You should get on the phone right now and tell Mr. Holman that you are not going to borrow his dog!" I was almost as convinced as she that she was right. As a rule of thumb that is nearly always the case, preternaturally.

A few weeks later I ran into Dawson at the Winn Dixie. He had a buggy full of dry dog food. I had four steaks, four Idaho potatoes and a six pack of beer. "Looks like you are feeding some fine dogs," he said with a Colgate grin after eyeing my buggy.

"Yes, your preacher and his wife are coming over for dinner," I joked, goading his Baptist constraints. "You got enough dog food to last you through the night?" I asked, pointing to the four fifty-pound sacks in his buggy.

"Doc," he said, "ole Rock loves this stuff. By the way, I'm expecting you and Paul to take him when you go to South Georgia." I muttered something about taking the responsibility of another man's dog and how I just would not feel comfortable doing it. "But Doc! I insist. Doc, you got to." He was getting louder and people were beginning to look our way, so I thanked him and hurried to the check out. Dawson was pertinacious and followed me to the car extolling the prowess of Rock and insisting that I be witness in South

Georgia to his best ever dog. He wheedled and cajoled as if his reputation were at stake. Somehow I avoided telling Ruth about the encounter.

Late one afternoon in early February, Dawson came by the office. My receptionist sent me word that he had come in "just to talk." I took a deep breath, knowing I was no match for him.

"Doc, do you have and electric collar?"

I said that I did.

"Well ole Rock has been hunting those pen-raised birds at Rock Fence, and, you know how they sometimes are hard to flush, he tends to creep some. You may need to touch him a couple of times with the shock collar, but that will stop his creeping." And he added, "Doc, he will do it all. Fine dog! He is one of the best I have ever had."

"I really am not comfortable taking your dog, Dawson. Maybe . . ."

"But Doc. I want you to take him. You won't have any trouble with him." Dawson was firm. I began to wonder how I would explain it to Ruth.

The night before the etesian event, I was cleaning my Superposed and packing my boots and other hunting gear. Ruth was sitting on the side of the bed watching intensely as if intrigued by my childish eagerness. All the while I was retelling some of the past adventures that happened in Early County. At first I thought she was paying attention.

"John," she said with a sigh. "I feel sorry for Leukos. You will bring him home full of cockleburs and sandspurs, and he won't move for a week because he will be so tired and stove up. I think hunting him like that is cruel."

"Oh," I said with relief, having the perfect opportunity to tell her the truth. "Actually, Dawson has so firmly insisted that I take his dog that I couldn't turn him down. He nearly broke down in tears when I finally agreed to take ole Rock. We'll probably hunt him and Leukos one at a time so as not to tire either one too much. Leukos will be alright. By the way, I trimmed him up this afternoon so as to avoid a lot of cocklebur dingle berries." I smiled at my wife, but she was not smiling back.

"What did I tell you about borrowing a dog to take to South Georgia?" It was not really a question. Ruth was not a kvetch, but she stuck to her point, convinced that she was right, even divinely inspired. "You're making a big mistake." She could just as well have added, "Thus saith the Lord God Almighty," and it would not have sounded more Deuteronomic.

I realized that I had lost the argument, just as I had lost the one with Dawson. It seemed that everything I said was so effete, so weak, and pointless; therefore, I changed the topic by telling her how much I was going to miss going to bed with her and snuggling up on a cold February night.

"You can snuggle with Dawson's dog she suggested," but managed a soft I'll miss you too smile. She then made a deep sigh, which I took to mean, "You are going to regret this!"

Paul knew the plan, and if he thought bad of it, he did not let on. We arrived at Dawson's house at daybreak, and as we entered the drive, the back porch light came on. Dawson was up, and with a smile full of teeth couldn't stop telling us how happy he was that we were taking ole Rock. "Doc, you and Paul are going to enjoy hunting with ole Rock, but be sure to put a shock collar on him, just to keep his attention."

"Dawson loves this damn dog," I finally said to Paul after we had driven in silence almost to Opelika.

"Yeah, and we are going to have to bring him back in fine condition," Paul said with a laugh. "He's got to be pristine."

"We must." I echoed, as the weight of the responsibility began to press hard upon my shoulders.

Paul changed the subject when we went through Pittsview, Alabama and began a long dissertation regarding an historic marker we passed. How he remembers all the minute details of the history of a remote rural community I'll never know. But Paul made it interesting—and long—and it took my mind off Dawson and his dog and Ruth's admonition.

We ate breakfast at the "pancake emporium," as Paul called it, in Eufaula, then crossed the Chattahoochee River back waters and headed south through Georgetown and Fort Gains toward Blakely. I had ordered our three day licenses on line, so it was not necessary to stop again until we got to William's.

Once more we found William and young friend, Toby, peering into the bed of Toby's truck. They both greeted us with an enthusiastic welcome. After the accustomed discussion about dogs and after relating the story regarding Dawson's dog, our attention was drawn to Toby's truck. Denver, his lab, was standing on the toolbox proudly keeping watch over the game in the bed of the truck. This time there were two ducks, a rabbit, a quail and several doves.

"Got these on the way over here," Toby said nonchalantly

"The season is out for ducks and doves," Paul objected. The protest only made William smile wider as if he were about to let us in on a joke of some sort. "Well?" asked Paul, sounding like someone's mother.

"It's out now, but was in earlier today," said Toby.

The afternoon hunt was productive of several pointed coveys, a number of missed shots—most of which resulted in roars of laughter from the Georgia boys—and half a dozen quail. Soon we were back at William's where Paul cleaned the birds while I took care of the dogs, and William and Toby busied themselves firing up the grill and enjoying a brew. Before long we were eating steak, properly blessed, and discussing the days hunt.

"Paul?" William drawled, his voice smiling and mischievous. Then there was a brief pause as if he wanted to make his question more dramatic, "Now

Sweet'n, didn't you tell me that you and the Doc had shot all the misses out of your guns?" He and Toby chuckled, grinning at each other as if it were some sort of private joke.

"Not all the misses," Paul said. "You were a witness to that."

"And the sad thing," I added, "is that it's the best we can do, and we are too old to improve." I was growing weary of the "shooting the misses out of your gun" gaff.

"Doc John, you just need to get yourself a real gun and you might be able to kill a bird," Toby joined in.

"Nothing wrong with the dang gun. I just don't have good hand eye coordination."

"And that is one fine dog you brought this time! He never pointed a bird that he didn't run up before we got within fifty yards of him," observed William.

"Yeah, well Dawson said he had some bad habits as a consequence of hunting pen-raised birds all the time. He wanted me to use the 'ole Alabama Power Company collar' and said that that would fix him, but I am not sure I can bring myself to shock another man's dog."

"Make me feel a lot better if you shocked the sombich," said William; "either that or leave him in the Jeep. If he were my dog, I would load up his ass with some number 8's, and that would stop him from flushing birds. Now Paul, the way things are going, you'd probably be better served if tomorrow we just drop you off over on Washington Street at the third house from the corner. Hell, then you won't have to worry about all the misses or Dawson's dog running up all the birds."

"Don't start that crap again, William." Paul should have known that it was no use to protest.

"And Paul, this ole girl is faster than that quail you were complaining about last year."

"And that is damn fast!" I interjected.

The next morning was overcast and warm for February. There was an eighty percent chance of rain. Toby had optioned to stay home, saying that his daughter, Bailey, was going to a birthday party and that he promised Brandi that he would stay with Alex, his two year old, till they got back. By the time we let the dogs down there were occasional sprinkles. Both dogs had on locator/shock collars. We put both Rock and Leukos down since it looked like the rain would make it a short hunt.

Before long Rock flushed a covey of birds and bounded off after them. The birds had been in a thin fence row at the crest of a hill and had flown down across a pasture into a swampy thicket. We chose to look for another covey and headed back for the Jeep. There began a light mist among the sprinkles. I blew my whistle, and Leukos came in and loaded immediately, but Rock was nowhere to be found. I turned on the locator collar, and we could hear a faint beep from across the pasture, a long way off. After fifteen minutes of whistling and listening, I became concerned and walked down the side of the hill, half way across the pasture. I could occasionally hear a faint beep. It began to rain.

"Hell, we're going to get wet," William growled. "How much do you think you would have to pay Dawson to leave that sombich here?"

"No, that won't do," I said, thinking of the potential disaster I faced. "Why don't you and Paul go get my truck before it really starts raining, and I'll stay here and try to get Rock?"

I heard the Jeep crank as I stood alone in the middle of the pasture on the side of the hill. The rain was coming hard now, and suddenly there was a flash and crash of lightning and thunder. I thought to myself how foolish it was to be standing in the open with a gun in my hands during a thunderstorm. If I got struck by lightning it would be no one's fault but mine, and the thought kept coming back, "maybe I deserve it." After all, the prophetess had spoken. I had a sickening, horrible feeling that Ruth was right as usual. As it is written, "He did that which was evil in the sight of the Lord, and the Lord struck him down." I could envision the report in the Alex City *Outlook*, "Local Physician Struck by Lightning in South Georgia Cow Pasture."

I couldn't hear the beeper at all now, so I fired a couple of shots hoping that it would bring Rock in. It didn't work. Rock continued to obstinately do whatever he was doing. I wondered if he was still in the same county. I began to think about how I could explain this to Dawson, and a deep sense of foreboding crept over my soul. I had never seen him angry, so I could only imagine his response. I weighed the question, "Which is worse, getting zapped by lightning or losing Dawson's best ever dog?"

Eventually, William and Paul reappeared on the crest of the hill as the rain eased to a light sprinkle. Suddenly we could hear the beeping of Rock's locator collar. Then he appeared, running along the edge of the swamp at bottom on the hill. Both William and I blew our whistles as loud as we could, but Rock took no notice. Reluctantly, I squeezed the button to shock him. The response was immediate; he turned and headed up the hill at a run. I was overwhelmed with joy! The bells of heaven began to ring, and the rain tapered to a fine misty drizzle. Then abruptly, he stopped some forty yards away, looked back down toward the swamp for a second, and started back.

"Shoot him, Doc!" screamed William. "Shoot that sombich! Shoot him!" He was nearly beside himself.

I raised my gun, but knew that I could not shoot another man's dog, not even with number 8's at forty yards. William was screaming frantically, "Shoot that sombich, Doc! Shoot him!" I pulled the control from my belt and pushed the shock button again. Rock's response was immediate, just like the first. He came on a dead run toward us. He ran past me and then past William, but Paul who was standing near the top of the hill just inside the pasture fence made a beautiful open field tackle and lay on top of the wriggling dog. Paul struggled to get a grip on his collar while not letting go of the hold he had, and then carried him all the way back to the truck and loaded him into the dog box.

"Damn dog is slippery!" said Paul.

"What in hell is that smell?" I asked as the rain started again. "I believe that dog has rolled in something bad. I have never smelled anything so bad!"

"The sombich has rolled in that dead cow in the swamp down there." William's face was red from screaming, or anger, or both. "Doc, if you had a' shot him like I told you, and you had stung him good, the sombich would have come back and loaded by himself, and Paul wouldn't have all this dead cow shit all over him."

"I think you just wanted me to shoot Dawson's dog," I said with a laugh. The situation was beyond ridiculous, and I felt such great relief that we would be returning Rock safely to Dawson that I was almost giddy.

"Would have made me feel a hell of a lot better," growled William, "a hell of a lot!"

The rain was coming down pretty hard again, but we road back to William's house in my truck with the windows down. Paul was covered with the slimy, stinking, dead cow gift from ole Rock. We hosed him off under the old pecan tree, and he undressed in the yard, spreading his clothes out on a barbed wire fence near the barn. We chained Rock to the pecan tree and hoped that the rain would wash him off a little. He stayed chained to the tree until we loaded up to come home.

"What are you going to tell Dawson about his dog?" Paul laughed as we arrived at Dawson's house.

"I'm going to say that I think he may have rolled in some stuff and that I noticed he tended to creep some, like he said."

"Yeah, he definitely has a tendency to creep!"

VII

O'Doul's

There were deer heads all around the walls in the grocery store in Fort Gains, Georgia. I have never seen anything like it in a place that sells food to cook, maybe in a barbeque joint or a sporting goods store. Paul and I stood there in amazement, gazing at the racks on the wall. We had shopped there before, but it was always fascinating.

"Looks like a frigging museum," I observed not realizing that Paul had gone ahead to commence shopping. No one responded. I hoped no one heard.

We got the sandwich makings, the salad makings, some nice potatoes and some snack foods and nibblings. We brought the steaks from home, not willing to take any chances with a store unfamiliar to us. "Let's get some beer. Looks like it's going to be another hot hunt," I said, more to myself than to Paul who would never be caught with a cold one in his Baptist hands.

"Why don't you?" was his surprising response. "I think that I'll get a six-pack of NAs."

"What?"

"NAs. You know, nonalcoholic beer, O'Doul's or the like."

"Paul, you can't drink that crap. Tastes like horse piss."

"So does the other stuff. At least I'll have something to sip on during the heat of the day while you guys are chugging the hard stuff." Once Paul's mind was made up about something, there was no changing it. I didn't bother to try.

"I'm buying this beer for Toby and William," I said weakly, knowing Paul knew better.

The rest of the way we retold William stories. Paul began to chuckle, "I can't wait for William to start that 'we'll drop you off at that old girls house' crap, because I am going to shut him up for sure."

"How's that?"

"Well, last fall after Mary Ann and I married, I brought her down here to meet William. She had heard all the stories and wanted to see him in person. I wanted William to meet her, too. So one Saturday we just got in the truck and rode down, taking a chance that we might find him at home, and sure enough he was home. We were sitting around the table talking when a car drove up to the back door, and this woman got out. She looked surprised to see us and didn't stay but a few minutes. I am not sure if William introduced us. She said that she lived in Fort Gaines and had come down to borrow a butcher knife. A butcher knife! I think she must be the one who is always cooking those pound cakes for William. When we left and started home, Mary Ann said, 'Paul, I'm no fool. No one drives twenty miles to borrow a butcher knife!' So I'll just say to Sweet'n when he tries to start all that crap, 'Can I borrow a butcher knife?'" Paul was more amused than I about the story, but I did not discourage his anticipated levity.

The afternoon was still fairly cool, and when the breeze picked up, it was a down right pleasant day to hunt. When we arrived at William's, Toby's Mule was parked in the back, his lab, Denver, sitting proudly on the box. The Mercury Cougar was in its rightful place under the carport. Contrary to Paul's prognostication, it hadn't died.

Toby met us at the kitchen door with a big smile and a loud welcome. He helped us bring in the groceries and our gear. I let the dogs out to stretch and fetched them some water. When I returned to the kitchen, the three were sitting at the old oak table talking about the dramatic escape we had made from the 'burning' Cougar. William was laughing, red faced and pointing at Toby. I heard Toby protesting as I walked in, "Naw! Naw! Paul. You thought we were on fire, too!"

So began a typical hunting adventure in Early County, Georgia. But there were some differences. For one thing, Paul and Mary Ann had married the preceding summer. This change would cramp William's style somewhat with the usual 'Now, Paul, I know this old girl' stuff. He would have to find another vulnerability to pick on. The second thing was that Toby was now an integral and essential part of our hunts, as was his Kawasaki Mule, and Denver. Our age differences did not matter, for with Toby along it was like hunting with one of my boys, and that always made things more exciting and more fun. No longer did he call Paul "Mister Paul" or me, "Doctor Blythe." From then on it was "Poolie" or "Paul" and "Doc John," or occasionally just "Doc." It was a good thing. The bad thing was William's health issue. He had spent several days in August in the hospital in Dothan and was not quite as perky as usual. Something was not quite right, but he seemed to not want to talk about it, and we did not press him. The other health issue was mine. I had enrolled in a study using an investigational drug to see if it would slow PSA progression. One of the side effects it had was severe nasal congestion. It had made me miserable; I did not sleep well and did not feel like my usual self. I spent the day with my mouth open and I struggled to work full time, but did. It was a hell of a price to pay to possibly keep the tiger away from the door a little longer.

Perhaps the biggest change was Belle, my Belle. She was a pretty little tricolor Llewellyn that I had had for nearly two years. This was her first real hunting season, and she was showing promise. I had been looking for a nearly all-white English setter when I ran across a litter of Llewellyn setters at a kennel near Clanton, Alabama. The goal was to find a mate for Leukos so as to maintain his blood line. Ruth was with me on the search, and she thought that Belle was the most beautiful puppy she had ever seen. Nothing would do but that we purchase her if for no other reason than to save her from what Ruth considered to be a puppy mill. We survived two heats and one puppy hunting season, and it seemed that the prospects were good for an interesting year. Belle and I bonded immediately. She loved to point quail wings dangling from and an old broken-tip fly rod and transferred that love to keeping a constant point on the fly as she accompanied me in the boat fishing. Standing on the bow seat, front legs slightly bent and tail tense and trembling, the hair feathering down like the trail of an Indian's war bonnet . . . she was a beauty to behold!

William's dogs had faded away a couple of years earlier. Leukos was showing his age and was not able to hunt more than half a day. It was sad to see him getting old and giving out, but I knew that William and I—and even Paul—were beginning to experience the same thing, though we tried to hide it.

"Doc John! Doc John!" Toby was more excited than usual. "Y'all brought a case of beer! But what is this O'Doul's stuff?"

"That's mine. I brought some NA so as to be sociable when you guys were doing your light sinning. So keep your hands off my O'Doul's."

"You don't have to worry about that," assured Toby.

"Now, Paul," began William. He always started that way when he began to rib him. "Just tell me how it is that you went and got married and Mary Ann won't even let you have a beer with the boys. Hell! I thought you were a Marine, a real man. Here you are married half a year and bad hen-pecked."

"No. That is not the way it is, Sweet'n. Y'all just drink what you want to drink, and I'll drink what I want."

"I'd as soon drink a bottle of cold piss." William began with a hard laugh that ended with a hard cough.

Paul and I excused ourselves to change into our hunting clothes and left Toby and William laughing in the kitchen. I came back to retrieve my boots which I had left at the carport door and found Toby busy as a cat with a caught mouse. He put a finger to his lips and said, "Shhh." He had slipped the caps off Paul's O'Doul's and was pouring them down the sink. He then refilled the bottles with beer and replaced the caps. I got the feeling that Toby had done this sort of thing before. I marveled at his skill and dexterity! "Don't tell Poolie!" he whispered. We could hear Paul singing in the back room while he covered his face and arms with sunscreen. William was smiling so widely, it looked like his face would bleed as he struggled to suppress laughter. His blue eyes darted from Toby to me and tears of delight trickled down his red cheeks. Old guys were enjoying a college prank.

Toby loaded up a large cooler with all Paul's O'Doul's and all the beer he could stuff in around the ice. "We're ready to go," he announced as Paul reentered the kitchen. "I've got your NA in the cooler, but I've got enough beer just in case you would prefer that."

"Let's go hunting. I've had enough of this beer crap. Doc, go load up the hounds."

"I got to have a cold one first," said William.

"Me too."

"And me too."

"Ok. This is probably a good time to try an O'Doul's," agreed Paul.

So we sat at the table another five minutes and toasted Belle, Leukos, Denver and the Kawasaki Mule. I thought William was going to bust. He and Toby would glance at each other and giggle like teenage girls at a school party.

"What's so blame funny?"

"Nothing," said Toby. "How's the O'Doul's?"

"It's ok. It really is. Now let's go hunting."

"You got on enough sunscreen? You smell like a banana." I inquired.

"I said, 'Let's go hunting!'" was Paul's response.

I do not know how fast a Mule will go with four men and three dogs and a dog box, but I feel sure that it was going as fast as it would go. Paul and I were on top and quickly got cold. I began with a light shirt, but had to make Toby stop so I could slip into my hunting coat. Paul pulled on the field jacket he still had from the Marine days. We stopped to make the usual round at the hog pen. William and Toby took the Mule to the dirt road, and Paul and I followed the dogs.

Leukos pointed first and Belle crept up behind him and honored. It was a beautiful sight, especially to me. The birds actually got up forty yards ahead in a thicket of small oak saplings. Neither of us got a shot. As expected the birds flew down the fence row and settled down. Paul took the road side. Toby got on the other side of the road about five yards beyond Paul. "I'm going to cover you, Poolie," he said carrying the 20 gauge Remington Model 1100 at his side.

The first bird flew down the fence row in the thicket and no one got a shot. The second one came my way, and I killed it on the second shot. I could not be sure what was happening on the other side of the fence row but heard shooting and excited voices from time to time. We met where the fence row played out into the edge of a peanut field. I had one bird, Paul had one and Toby had three. "How the hell did that happen?" I asked.

"Toby is just too damn fast," said Paul in a somewhat subdued tone.

We were midway through the debriefing when a black pick up rode up and stopped. The driver shut off the motor and looking at William said, "You are not supposed to be hunting on my side of the road, Hudspeth."

"We weren't hunting on your place, Fred, goddammit!"

"I saw somebody kill a bird over here. I saw that lab go fetch it."

"I shot the bird in the middle of the road, Fred. It got up on William's side. Whose damn bird do you think it is?" Toby was holding his own.

"I'm just telling you not to be hunting on my property." Fred cranked up and scowled at Paul and me.

"Nice to meet you," I said not meaning to sound sarcastic.

The truck disappeared in a blaze of dust. "Who was that?" asked Paul.

"That was the infamous Fred Saunders," said Toby.

"Biggest son of a bitch in Early County," William added. "Owns a lot of land that joins me and is always accusing me of poaching on his. Used to let me hunt it but got mad about something a few years ago and has been an asshole since. One time he even called the sheriff because we were shooting singles that had landed on his side of the road."

"Let's have a beer and go over to the pond," suggested Toby as he handed Paul an O'Doul's and William and me a beer.

The pond was just across the road from William's house. It had been used for stock watering years ago, but was pretty well grown up with all sorts of vines and bushes. Some parts had been kept open by mowing and disking and some were under some large oaks which at one time were at the water's edge. We had been hunting a short while when one of the dogs ran up a covey. The singles flew to the south side of the pond and settled between it and an old fence where there were a few scattered large oaks and one of the areas that had been strip disked in the late summer. A couple of deer stands were located along the fence facing the pond.

Paul and I took our positions, he along the edge of the fence and I just above the wet edge of the pond. William and Toby were behind us in the Mule, easing along as we walked. We each killed a bird, and we each missed one. We were nearly to the end of the walk when a bird got up just in front of me. It crossed left to right, an awkward shot for me, but I managed to bring it down the second shot. It was not killed clean and began to run as we approached. I was still in the process of reloading so it was reassuring to hear Toby shoot. I hate to have a crippled bird escape.

"Want another O'Doul's? Toby shouted to Paul as he joined us at the Mule.

"No. I'll just have one with supper. They are ok actually. You guys can kid me if you want to." Paul glanced at William who was laughing and coughing and slapping his knees.

As I was about to mount to the top seat, William grabbed my leg and whispered, "Let's tell him, Doc. What do you say?"

"Not now, William. Not now," somehow it seemed that I was in charge of the caper.

In the cool of the evening, we sat at the old oak table. We ate salad, potatoes, bread and steaks that we had cooked in the carport on the truck-rim grill, and we all had another beer, though Paul didn't know it.

Paul went to the carport to give the dogs some steak scraps, leaving the three of us at the table, giggling like children. "Doc, let's tell him!" insisted William as Toby nodded his agreement.

"No. Not yet. Just wait."

The next morning was perfect, cool and sunny. There was a minimum breeze. The daffodils and paper whites were blooming all over William's yard. There were pale pink blooms on the plum trees over by the dog pen and the tulip tree—or whatever it was—was almost in full bloom. There were almost two more weeks in February, but spring was on its way, ground hog to the contrary not withstanding.

I was feeding the dogs when Toby drove up in his truck, Denver on the tool box and a pretty little dark haired girl in his lap. "This is Bailey," he said as he introduced us. "I'm taking her to her granddad's house, and then I'll be back with the Mule."

"Hi, Bailey. Can you believe that I have a granddaughter about your age, and her name is Bailey, too? I will surely remember your name. And I will remember you because you are such a pretty thing."

"Thank you," she said demurely as they departed. She was a strikingly pretty little girl. I worried about her riding in her daddy's lap.

Paul and I were atop the dog box on the Mule and were wearing our field coats in anticipation of the windy ride. William and Toby were snickering and joking as they loaded the cooler. They took turns taking jabs at Paul and his O'Doul's. Each of them gave me a glance and a wink as they took their seats, simpering like school girls. Denver was sitting between Paul and me. It was a beautiful, bright, cool and crisp South Georgia day. All was right with the world; we were bird hunting!

The morning was great. The dogs hunted fairly close and took their time. They held their points and retrieved the down birds, Denver getting her share. One point was particularly picturesque: At the edge of a peanut field in cover mostly of buffalo grass and sedge Belle pointed and Leukos backed. Belle's Llewellyn tricolors were brilliant in the morning sun. She was beautiful! Leukos stood staunch with head high and tail upright. The light breeze made the feathered hair on his tail undulate like a parade flag. He looked whiter than usual, really classy, reminding me of the picture of Mr. Thor I had cut out of the *American Field* magazine. Neither dog moved till the birds bursts out of the grass between them. They all came up simultaneously creating a roar and a vision whose memory would bring tears to the eyes of any true bird hunter, and confusion, uncertainty and vacillation to the shooter. We did our best, and William and Toby nodded their approval. So the morning went. After a sandwich and beer at William's, we remounted the Mule and began the afternoon foray.

I cannot remember every covey or every single, and I cannot remember every time Toby shot while sitting in the Mule. I do remember that the afternoon grew warm and less productive. Leukos looked fatigued and spent most of the time in the box aboard the Mule.

After one particularly hard round through a conservation easement and recreated wetland that was overgrown in briars and vines, Paul and I racked our guns and reached for the cooler. Toby and William, currently enjoying refreshment, were especially interested in our activity. Paul snapped the cap from his O'Doul's and settled in the shade of a small pine tree. The two pranksters glanced at each other grinning with anticipation. "Doc John, let's tell him. Ok?"

"Not yet, Toby." It was unclear how I became in charge of the japery.

"Doc, let's tell him," implored William. They were beginning to sound almost child like.

Then, as if on cue, Paul burst out, "Good Gosh! I've had all the O'Doul's I can stand. These things make you fart like a race horse!"

William grasped his sides nearly falling out of the Mule. Laughing, wheezing and coughing, he gasped to speak, but couldn't. Toby was dancing around pointing at the cooler and shouting at me, "Doc John, we got to tell him."

"Yeah. Now is a good time; you'd better tell him," I said.

VIII

Argentina

We all gathered at the tractor shed on the east side of the big field. At one time this had been a home site, and remnants of the old chimney and some of the foundation stones remained as witness to by gone times. The two hollow oaks also remained, barely still surviving the rough years, and offering little shade from the September sun. A variety of pickup trucks and two cars crowded near the shed which housed a Ford 3000 tractor, several five-gallon buckets of diesel fuel and other farming essentials. The gathering looked like a small family reunion. There were a dozen of us telling jokes and reminiscing about opening day dove shoots in the past, while several of the younger guys kept watch on the power lines that crossed the big field. It had been disked and smoothed with a drag and planted in wheat, top sewn. There was no need to be in a hurry. The doves always began collecting on the wire long before they flew the field, and if this year was like the preceding fifteen or so, there would be plenty of opportunities to shoot.

The usual gang was there: Paul and Al, my sons Bill and Brian, Al's son, John, my old bird hunting partner Mike, Robert the Chevy Dealer and friend since first grade, and several others equally willing to dawdle away an afternoon. There was plenty of talk about the old days when the seniors of the group were young men and the second generation was still in diapers. We told stories of hot days in September, of great shoots and misadventures of all sorts. There was the one about the rattlesnake that ate the bird one of the guys was looking for in high grass, and how the bird was retrieved by milking it retrograde from the headless serpent. There were exaggerated tales of consumption of quantities of beer during and after shoots, something definitely off limits now. Most of all we talked about the annual dove suppers which invariably resulted in some degree of debauchery, reprimand, and spousal retaliation. Some of the stories were told in hushed voices to be out of ear shot from the younger bunch so as not to corrupt them with ideas they might glen from the epics. Those days were long gone leaving only their memories to be amplified, embellished and glorified.

About the time when Mickey's short hand pointed at three and the long hand at twelve, there developed a consensus to go afield. Soon the first bunch of doves ventured to fly the field, resulting in considerable gunfire, mostly futile. This continued through out the afternoon frequently enough to keep everyone's attention, except for the brief public announcements when someone with a portable radio would report the latest score of the Auburn game. It was a fine day to shoot doves and an even better day to rehydrate at the end of the shoot, gathered around a selected tail gait while "pulling" the doves.

"We should invite William and Toby to shoot with us sometime," Paul suggested as we were about to ride off into the sunset. "Seems like we usually have a good shoot around opening day every year."

"Yeah, that's a good idea. We'll see what they say about driving up for a shoot," I said cautiously, for the one thing I didn't want to do was to invite them up and we not have many doves. I always planned weekend shoots on Wednesdays for that very reason.

It is funny how time flies and seasons go. Almost before we knew it February was nearly gone and we were sitting around the old oak table in William's kitchen drinking iced tea and eating ham sandwiches, all duly and properly blessed. It was clear that there had been "choir practice" the night before for the cards and poker chips were still on the table. The initial conversation was general stuff, the same as always happens when old friends covey up. First, you ask polite things and give vague generic answers that are totally meaningless and reserved. Then someone breaks the ice, so to speak. This time, it was Paul who got William talking, "Well, William, I see that you have had choir practice again. What else have you been up to?"

Ignoring the discovery of the cards, he said. "I've been planning on your coming down here to hunt with me. I've been making preparation. Now, Paul . . ."

("Oh, hell! Here it comes," I thought.)

"Now, Paul, I've got this arrangement worked out with this ole girl, so you won't need to get your gun out . . . I mean your metal one. The Doc and I, and Toby, if he ever gets here, will just hunt by ourselves. She don't live far from here, so you can just take the old Cougar and come on back when you've had all you can stand . . ."

Red faced, Paul was shaking his head, not so much in response to William's plan, or the certainty that there would be no such peccadillo, as much as in resignation to the fact that he kept suggesting it. "Be kind, William, and don't start that crap again."

"Paul, I'm just trying to help you out: just want you to have some good ole South Georgia fun. Hell, I am being kind. Besides you probably haven't shot all the misses out of your guns like I told you. Have you? Have you, Doc?"

"I shot a good many out during dove season, but there are likely a good many left." I answered, sort of for us both. "We haven't seen enough quail to shoot many misses."

Our conversation was interrupted by the sound of truck tires on the gravel drive. It was Toby arriving in his crew cab Chevy with his yellow lab, Denver, atop the tool box.

"Sorry I'm late," he said as he joined us at the table, having poured himself a glass of tea. "Woody has got two crews working on the same track of timber and they are fighting over the chip-and-saw. Hell, they were about to have it out in the middle of the woods, and I had to go get things settled before somebody got cut."

"You ain't late, Toby," William said disregarding the timber dilemma. "I'm just now giving Paul his instructions about this afternoon."

"You mean you got Mr. Paul fixed up again?"

"He has *never* had me fixed up, Toby. You know that."

"That's not what he tells me, Mr. Paul." Toby knew how the game was played, and had joined right in.

"Well, don't believe any of William's prevarications. He always says the same thing. Just blowing smoke, you know."

"This time he's not, Mr. Paul. I heard him on the phone yesterday talking to one of his lady friends and describing you in detail. He even asked her 'please.' Said that you'd be slicked down and lathered up and smelling like you just came from the beach." Toby continued with a description of the alleged phone call while William laughed and slapped his knee, finally progressing into a convulsion of coughing.

"Why, hell, Paul," William said between spasms of laughter and coughing, "I'm just trying to keep you from having, as the lawyers say, 'loss of consortium.' But maybe if you don't have no consortium, you can't have no loss of it."

"Why don't we just go hunting?" Paul demanded.

We proceeded after some delay to a slash pine plantation of about forty acres which was surrounded on all sides by crop fields. Three of the sides had been in cotton the year before, and the stubble had been mowed and the fields recently disked. The other field was in milo, and the grain was still standing, not having been combined, because, according to William, it takes so long for milo to dry in the field. The slash plantation was not a pretty site. It had been planted eighteen years earlier and had not done well because of severe competition in its first several years. Later a storm of some sort had broken much of it down, and there had been a lot of pine beetle damage. A prescribe fire had cleaned it up to a degree making it ideal habitat for rabbits and deer. There was a lot of down fall, so the walking was rough.

William and Toby let us out on the west side of the plantation and promised to meet us on the opposite side beyond a drainage ditch which they could get to only by going back to the main road and coming in from the east. Paul and I were to hunt the edge counter clockwise and commenced to do so as they left. Soon after starting we walked up a covey of birds that flew to the interior of the plantation. We both shot out of desperation but did not score. We managed to scare up some of the singles, most of which were not pointed, and none of which were killed. As we proceeded back to the edge, Leukos pointed another large covey which got up ahead of us and out of range. We found singles out of that covey, too, but did not kill any. The trees and hanging vines made seeing the birds difficult and hitting them almost impossible. I saw two of my loads bust the bark off trees nowhere near where I needed to have shot. Walking became more and more problematic because of the dense boot-grabbing vines, the stump holes and the down falls. Eventually we reached the east side of the thicket, exhausted, thirsty, and without game. William and Toby were waiting as planned beyond a deep drainage ditch which had steep sides and standing water in the bottom. The crossing place I chose was far from ideal. I wound up sliding boot first into the bottom and after several attempts managed to extricate my soaked self from the other side. Paul crossed at another point a hundred yards or so to my left and emerged unscathed and dry.

William found the adventure hilarious, and took great joy at my appearance and obvious exhaustion. "Hell, Doc, why didn't you just jump that little ole ditch like Paul did. Look at him, he ain't wet, and he don't look to be as white eyed as you. He must have made you walk through the honey suckle while he walked the trail . . ."

"What damn trail are you talking about? We didn't see a trail," I demanded.

"I'm talking about the trail we ride when we are rabbit hunting that place," William said, sounding almost serious. "Sure 'nuf there is a trail that would have brought you to the foot bridge over the ditch."

"Why in the living dog shit didn't you tell us about that? I thought I was going to drown in that frigging ditch. The water was up past my butt. I didn't think I was ever going to get out, the bank was so steep and slickly."

"We heard you shooting. How many birds did you kill?" William was grinning widely as he took a huge chew of Red Man.

Neither of us answered. "I'm taking off these damn boots and squeezing the water out of my socks," I finally said jumping with what strength remained on the tail gait of Toby's truck.

"I know I heard y'all shooting a dozen or more times, Mr. Paul," Toby joined in. "Don't tell me you did not kill a bird."

"Not a bird; not in that jungle."

"You boys get some water, and let's hunt the bottom of the draw where this ditch opens up at the end of that milo," suggested William, "that is, if you are not too worn out. Doc was scratching and sliding like a rat in a slop jar."

"I'm ok. Just let me get my boots back on," I said taking my time and drinking two more cups of water. "And let me be sure I've got all the mud out of my gun."

We hunted the draw as William suggested, finding another large covey. Paul killed one bird, but I missed both shots, again. The singles were unkind, as were the comments of Toby and William. We ended the afternoon with only one bird.

"I'm sure you won't need any help cleaning that one bird," I said to Paul as we returned to William's house. "I'm getting out of these wet pants and boots and am going to take a shower."

"If you ain't one pitiful-looking, old wore-out bird hunting, broken-down old shad, Doc," said William. "Yeah, you better get your sorry ass on in and get cleaned up. Hell, you look worse than ole Leukos did the first year you hunted him down here, hair all full of cockleburs and sandspurs and walking straddle-legged."

"I couldn't be more miserable if I had cockleburs in my short hair," I said with only minimal exaggeration. "How about y'all having the steaks on when I get back; at least my appetite is ok."

"Fire up the grill, Toby. Let's make the Doc happy he came down even though he got wet and didn't kill any birds. I'm going to find some brown water so he can have, as he says, and 'attitude adjustment' after he gets cleaned up."

"First good idea you've had all day, William," I said as I tossed my wet boots under the Mercury Cougar and draped my socks over the side of the back steps.

Toby made a fire in the homemade tire rim grill using a couple of splinters of fat wood, or as we call it in Alabama, "lighter." Before long he had the charcoal burning and had brush-cleaned the grate. As soon as the coals began to glow, he tossed in among them four foil-wrapped Idaho potatoes. Paul handed him the inch and a quarter thick rib eye steaks, cautioning him to not let any get past medium rare, and then busied himself with the salad and bread. William set the table and jabbed at Paul about his shooting skills, or lack thereof. I took a warm shower.

Shortly, all was ready, and we settled down around the old oak kitchen table and thanked the Almighty for the good food and the fellowship of good friends. No one mentioned to Him the brown water on account of the possibility of its interdiction, should God be Baptist. In all honesty, William and I were not hypocritical about it; nor did we pretend to take of it for our stomachs' sake. It was the twilight of a great day, and I think the Lord looked on it and said it was good.

"William," I said as we finished eating, "Paul and I want you and Toby to come to one of our dove shoots. Sometimes we have quite a few doves, but probably not like you have down here. We would like for you to come just the same and enjoy some Alabama hospitality."

"We might come sometimes," said Toby. "I killed the limit every time I shot this year, which was about four times a week. We had more doves than I can remember."

"Hell, let me tell you about the time I went to Argentina dove hunting with a couple of buddies from the co-op." William cleared his throat, and we knew from his tone that we were about to hear a tale. "Before we left I went down to Parker's Drug Store and got a dozen Trojan rubbers so I would be prepared. Now Paul, we shot a lot of doves. I shot more than two cases of shells during the three days we were there. Had these native kids: one loading the extra gun, one fetching doves, and one holding my beer while I shot. There were doves everywhere, coming in by the hundreds. Never seen anything like it.

"I got back to the hotel, took me a long hot shower, and we went out for a steak. I told the bell boy on the way out that we needed some women, one each. I gave him twenty dollars, and when we got back there were three fine looking young Spanish women waiting for us. He sent one to my room, and man was she fine: tall, thin, with huge firm tits and a nice round ass . . ." He continued in detail about the pulchritude of the woman, leaving no detail of her physiognomy to the imagination. "I had given my buddies some Trojans, and I slipped one on, and, let me tell you, Paul, I was doing some pretty work. And she was enjoying it too, hollering and screaming in Spanish, speaking in tongues, or something. Oh, she was fine! And I could feel that poison coming down the back of my neck to both sides of my groins, drawing my toes up into little fists, and I could feel my prostrates busting. When we finally got finished and I got the strength and breath to get up, I looked down, and all I had on was a damn O-ring. The rest of that Trojan rubber was gone, burnt off or blown off or something. It's a wonder I hadn't come home with the bull-headed clap or something worse."

"We don't believe a word of that, William," said Paul as William rolled out of his chair in laughter, all the time pointing at him as if the joke was on Paul. "You're just trying to hornswoggle us."

"Now, Paul . . ." William could not talk for laughing and coughing. He was proud of the canard he had crafted, but his laughter was spoiling his punch line. We were all laughing at the ribald humor, though it was not the story so much as the way he told it that made it risible.

"And, William," I broke in with my best clinical voice. "It's *prostate*, not *prostrate*. One is a gland, the other a position. Sounds like you are trying to describe a prostate busting frisson."

"Yeah, and I was talking about them both, Doc, doing some prostrate busting frigging."

"Be nice, William."

"I'm going to have a dram of nostrum on that one. William, you've probably had enough."

IX

Snakes

William demonstrated the knot for the fourth time and handed the bait casting rod to me. "Now Doc, if you can't tie a knot that will hold your lure on, how can you sew somebody up?"

"I don't," I said sharply. "I don't cut on people, so I don't have to sew them up, just like I don't deliver babies or treat children. That is not what I do for a living. I never have been good at tying knots, not even when I was a Boy Scout."

"Just do as I tell you then," he said, bringing back a rush of unpleasant memories of my first encounter with a surgery resident when I was a third year medical student. "Put the line through the eye and make a loop. Then go back through the eye the opposite way. Bring the loop around the line and make a simple over-hand knot, leaving everything loose. Now go over the lure with the loop . . . Damn! Doc, you got anything other than thumbs? Now tighten up on your knot . . . Doc, Hell!"

"What's wrong with this knot?" I asked defiantly. "I thought I demonstrated exceptional bimanual dexterity."

"For one thing, it's not right."

"Y'all put that crap down and let's go hunting." Paul had been patient for as long as he could stand it. "Even if you learn to tie it, you won't remember it come fishing time. This is an absolute waste of time!"

"What is the difference in a waste of time and an absolute waste of time?" I asked without looking up.

"One is absolute. Come on; we came down here to bird hunt. You can demonstrate your dexterity with your fowling piece."

"Now, Paul . . ." We knew what to expect when William began this way. "The Doc and I are busy, but we can drop you off at this ole girl's place and come get you when I get through teaching the Doc how to tie knots. Hell, Doc, you are going to enjoy fishing once you learn to tie your bait on."

Toby had been quietly observing the scene from the front fender of the Cougar, grinning and chuckling like he thought old folks were funny. "I'm with Mr. Paul: we're wasting valuable hunting time. I say, lets go hunting, and we can drop Mr. Paul off on the way, if that's what he wants."

"Toby, don't you start that crap, too! You've been hanging out with William too much. He's corrupting your youth." Paul didn't sound prudish.

We did not persist with the lesson and soon were aboard Toby's Kawasaki Mule, dogs and all. Denver, the lab, sat behind and between Paul and me, atop the dog box. Belle and Leukos were in the box, both panting and salivating with anticipation.

The mid-afternoon sun was warm for February; it was a 'one shirt day' in Early County, Georgia. There were a few high cumulous clouds which gave intermittent reprieve from the rays, and the wind was occasionally gusty, but there was no real abatement from the heat. Paul and I were both sweating profusely when we returned from the first put-down, and began to wonder if perhaps we should have continued with the knot tying a while longer. Toby, William, and Denver were observing our travail from the Mule in the shade of an ancient water oak and indicated no concern for our distress.

"Y'all didn't find any quail birds, Mr. Paul?" It wasn't clear if Toby was asking, observing or taunting.

"Did you hear us shoot? You and William sitting back here in the cool of the shade just watching the Doc and me . . . don't ask any dumb questions."

"If you'd take off those snake leggings, you wouldn't be so hot, and the walking would be a lot easier." I ventured.

"You can get snake bit if you want, John, but I'm keeping these on in this hot weather. The way things are going, snakes may be all we see."

"I don't recall us ever seeing one down here. Do you?"

"No, but I don't want the first one I see to be the one that bites me." Paul had applied a lavish amount of sunscreen on his face, and the sweat was creating little stripes down his face.

"Ain't no snake that wants to bite your sorry ass, Paul," William broke in, as he took a big chew of Red Man. "Besides, if one did, you got a doctor right with you."

"I don't do snake bites," I said as I poured some water for the dogs.

"To be so bimanual, you don't do much of anything, do you Doc?" William was on the attack.

"Yeah, I also don't sit my ass in the shade and let somebody else do all the walking."

"Toby and I were letting you and Paul get warmed up. We're going to have a beer, want one."

"Not while we're hunting," I spoke for both of us. "Water is fine."

We moved on to a soy bean field and hunted the edge. Paul and I walked on either side of the fence row, working the dogs all the way to the toe of the field where it narrowed at an old hog lot that had usually been productive of one or two coveys. This was one of two old hog lots that we hunted regularly when at Williams. They were a mile or more apart and had little in common except that they were grown up and were near a lot of cultivated ground. As we crossed the narrow end, we could still see scattered beans on the ground that had persisted through the winter. There were also many turkey tracks, unsurprisingly.

Before we reached the other side, we could see the dogs pointed just over the fence. Toby had driven the Mule down to the corner of the fence, just below where they were pointed, and having loaded up was standing ready to shoot anything that ventured to attempt a field crossing. William, as usual, was monitoring from the Mule. Paul entered the lot through a gap almost directly behind the dogs as I attempted to cross ten yards to his left at a point where the hog-wire fence was nearly down. One pays little attention to briars or pain when the dogs are pointed, and when I finally escaped their concertina wire like bondage, the backs of both my hands were bleeding. As I got up even with Paul, the birds erupted in a bustling commotion, a confusing, crisscrossing flurry of madness, frantic wings pounding breasts with rapid hammering blows. The first bird I selected turned right toward Paul; abandoning it, I fired away at one that crossed my way just behind it. It fell and I dropped a second one going straight away. Paul doubled also. None of them tried to fly the field, so Toby did not shoot. It took some time to fetch up the four downed birds, but with persistence we were able to pocket all of them, with little help from the hyper-excited dogs. While we waited for the singles to settle and create scent, we went back to the Mule to report to William.

"Did Paul shoot you, Doc?" he asked as we approached.

"No. Why?"

"You look like you been shot; you got blood all over your face and shirt. Or, were y'all fighting over there?" William had opened another beer and was purposely not commenting on our perfect shooting.

Running my hand across my face, I instantly knew why he asked about being shot. I could feel the sting of the briar scratches on my bloody and sweaty cheeks. In the excitement I had not noticed when it occurred. I took a folded paper towel from my pocket and wiped and blotted until William confirmed that all was mopped up.

As we were about to commence the single hunting, William cautioned, "You boys need to hunt all the way to the end of the field, on past the old slop pens to the road."

"Yes, Bwana." I tipped my cap as we returned to the over grown lot to resume.

We found Leukos on point almost immediately. The single flew Paul's way, and he killed it. We downed two more and missed another as we worked our way up the tangles of the old pen. As we approached the remains of a wooden fence and scattered pieces of corrugated tin roofing that had once been part of a farrowing pen, the area narrowed, so I crossed the fence to the edge of the field as Paul forged straight ahead. Suddenly there was a gasp. I could see Paul in an instant jumping backward and simultaneously shooting toward the ground immediately in front of him. At the same time I saw a snake in clear sight that had jumped above the level of the weeds and grass. I hurried over to Paul who was open-mouthed and speechless, for a moment. "Gosh! I'm glad I had these snake gaiters on! That damned thing could have bit me, and it's a cotton mouth."

"And that's a big snake! It jumped clear off the ground when you shot it." The snake was still writhing as I used the butt of my shotgun to hold its head down while cutting it off with my knife. "This is the only poisonous snake we have seen hunting down here."

"You mean the *first* one! I told you that you ought to be wearing leggings, too."

"I just watch where I step."

William and Toby were watching the commotion from the Mule and were anxious to hear the particulars and, naturally, wanted to see the headless reptile. We gathered around the deceased ophidian which Toby had fetched from the hog pen. Paul recreated the kerfuffle with the gusto of a second grader doing a show and tell. We loaded the dogs and our guns, mounted the Mule and moved up toward the road where the hog yard ended, a distance of ten yards or less. As we approached the road, two quail flushed from the edge of the road.

"I thought I told you to hunt the entire pen, up to the road!" roared William.

Paul and I looked at each other. "We should have followed his guidance," Paul conceded.

We took a break, let the dogs down at a pond to indulge in a wallow and drink, and then stopped off at Mrs. Saunders' grocery. An anachronism somehow preserved, it was like a Model A still running, old and quaint but serving a needed function in rural Early County. It was a filling station, grocery and general merchandise all in one. There were a few essential groceries, like sardines and crackers and packages of peanuts, Moon Pies, and cheese crackers. It also had other essentials like chewing tobacco and cold drinks. Paul and I downed a couple of Big Orange drinks, while Toby bought another six-pack of Bud for himself and William, the two having somehow worked up a tremendous thirst.

Mrs. Saunders was a small woman a decade or more beyond retirement age. She had run the store for years and had known Toby and William almost forever. Her voice was unique but strangely familiar—nasally, high pitched and scratchy, sort of irritating like. She spoke a slow, deeply Southern, bucolic drawl that sounded almost contrived. I felt sure that I had heard her voice before but couldn't place where. It was *deja vu* almost, and I couldn't stop thinking and wondering about her the rest of the afternoon. But later that evening, after we had showered and dressed for our traditional trip to the mullet house, and were sitting around the old oak kitchen table recapitulating the day's adventure, it came to me. Suddenly the recollection was as clear as the conversation we were having, so before we departed for dinner, I felt compelled to tell them the story.

Early one morning several years back the phone ringing awakened me from a sound sleep. The night was beginning to lighten a bit, hinting that dawn was near, but the sun was not even close to being up.

"Doctor Blair?"

"No, this is Doctor *Blythe*." I cleared the sleep from my throat and tried to speak clearly.

"Doctor Blair, this here is Etoye Westerfield, Doctor Blair."

"I'm Doctor *Blythe*." I knew that there was no Dr. Blair in town and didn't try again to correct her.

"Well, Doctor Blair, I'm calling about my husband, Cletus, Doctor Blair."

"What's the problem?"

"Well, Doctor Blair, Cletus needs hisself a doctor, Doctor Blair. He goes to the Veteran's Hospital down at Tuskegee, but he needs him a home doctor." I could hear the rooster crowing in the background.

"I'm not sure . . . I . . . uh . . . understand." What I did understand was that this was one situation I wanted to avoid.

"Doctor Blair, we've heared good saying on you, and we want you to be Cletus' doctor."

"Mrs. Westerfield, I'm an oncologist; I treat patients with cancer. Does your husband have cancer?"

"No, Doctor Blair. All's wrong with Cletus is that he is a dope feign and a alcoholic, Doctor Blair." It sounded like she was saying "alke-hall-ic."

"It doesn't sound like he has the kind of problem that I treat." I was now wide awake and glanced at the alarm clock: 4:45.

"What am I going to do with Cletus, Doctor Blair?"

"Why don't you take him to Doctor Warr? I think he treats stuff like that." I immediately felt a twinge of guilt because that wasn't true. As a matter of fact I knew it was plain wrong, but I still owed him one for April Fool's Day, and I was being tempted above that which I was able.

"You think Doctor Warr will see him? He's just a dope feign and a alcoholic, Doctor Blair."

"Just tell his secretary that I recommended Doctor Warr to you, and tell her that he has stomach trouble. That'll get you in." It was all I could do to keep from laughing out loud. Lloyd Warr is a gastroenterologist and my friend, my mentor, and the man who covers for me when I'm out of town. But he is also the man who sent the hyperventilating teenager to my office, telling her I specialized in her kind of problem. He called me later on that afternoon from his office and said, "April fool!" and hung up. It was get even time.

The next day, I took my seat at the long table in the back of the hospital cafeteria where as a longstanding tradition several of the doctors enjoyed each other's company and exchanged stories or hashed out patient problems at the noon meal. I had not been there long when my esteemed colleague arrived. I tried not to look guilty or to smile, so when he put his tray down across the table from me, I didn't look up. "Blythe," he said with a voice of righteous indignation, "you sombich, you!"

I knew my sins were about to be revealed. "What's the problem, Bubba?" I began calling him 'Bubba' years earlier when I discovered that it was his mother's affectionate name for him. She reverted to calling him by it when she became old.

"Damn your eyes." By this time he had the attention of everyone at the table. "I know it was you that set me up with Cletus Westerfield."

"Who? What are you talking about, Bubba?" I tried to be as grandiloquent as possible.

"Yeah! He said you told him to say he has stomach trouble. The only thing wrong with his stomach is the stuff he pours into it, and by that criterion he has mouth and esophagus trouble, too."

"All that's your specialty, isn't it?" By this time all the brethren were enjoying the entertainment. I continued to dance around, and he proceeded to unwind the story.

Finally, after a long gulp of tea, he said, with his eyes glaring below his frizzley eyebrows, "I'll get you for this."

Several weeks later as I was about to leave my office for lunch at the hospital cafeteria, I got a call from the hospital lab. "Doctor Blythe, we need your help with a blood slide on one of Doctor Warr's patients, can you come by on your way to lunch?"

I said "sure" and stopped by the laboratory to look at the blood film. It was the most bizarre-looking blood I had ever seen; there were large funky-looking nucleated red blood cells, numerous immature-looking white cells, and variously shaped platelets. "What is this?" I wondered, and then noticed several lab techs watching me attentively and snickering. I studied the name on the slide to see if it was a patient I recognized. The label read, "Chickadee Williams." "Ah, yes!" I said out loud. "Where the hell did you get this chicken blood?" I asked the techs, who readily confirmed my suspicion.

Lloyd was already seated at the end of the long table, and it was obvious that he had explained the set up to the accustomed assembly of colleagues. He said nothing about the slide and didn't ask any questions, and I stonewalled him. Finally, as the lunch hour was about to end, Doctor Watwood, peered over his glasses and asked, "What did you think about that blood film."

"It was chicken blood," I said. "Bubba was trying to set me up."

"What makes you think it was me?" He didn't sound the least bit innocent.

"You're the only chicken frigger around. That's why."

Having related the caper, I explained that it was Mrs. Saunders' voice that brought to mind Etoye Westerfield and the adventures of Cletus. "It's strange how people sound alike," I said. "It took me a while to remember who she sounded like."

"We've heared good saying on you, too, Doc," said William.

X

Days of Grass

Seale, Alabama is a small out of the way town which, I think, at one time was the County Seat of Russell County. Paul explained it all to me in great detail again. He had done so on almost every trip to Early County, but I have never been good at history and quickly forgot most of the story. The main thing I remembered about Seale was that the rail road overpass was too low for trucks to go under, so they had to detour down town. Another bypass had been in the works for several years and soon Seale and the old county seat and the low bridge would no longer remind travelers of those bygone days. It did get my mind off a bad subject and injected conversation into a quiet ride. Most of our discussion had been about taking four dogs in a Yukon and blaming each other whenever one passed an unusually foul flatus. Given the other issue, the dogs riding inside the vehicle with us was not a painful subject.

We were concerned about William's health and especially how he would tolerate less than pleasant weather. William had insisted that we make the trip, reassuring us that he was ok and that the cold front would not be an issue. He would put Toby in charge, and if it got too rough, he would just go to the house and wait for us.

The whole thing made me uneasy. It was never clear to me just what William's health problem was or what had happened to him the previous summer. My physician's curiosity was not satisfied with vague explanations. "His sister told me that he had had some sort of spell which was at first thought to be some kind of a stroke and that he had been in the hospital in Dothan," Paul explained when he called to break the news in September. Some type of surgery was planned but then cancelled. He had gradually gotten better but was still having "problems."

Paul and Mary Ann had visited him in October, and their observation was that William seemed a little subdued but looked ok generally; however, something wasn't right. Phone conversations were not very reassuring for there was something about his voice, like a singer a little off key, or maybe it was what he didn't say. One thing was sure: he wanted us there; he insisted that we come. And we wanted to be there. It was not that it was an etesian event, an annual tradition, and certainly hunting was not important any more, just an excuse to go.

We had made a mutual concession with William that Paul and I would stay at a motel in Blakely, and we agreed not to hunt Sunday. William had enjoyed the solitude of living off the back roads of South Georgia and had enjoyed company when he wanted it, but following the hospitalization in Dothan his siblings had insisted that he not be alone at night in case he had another "spell," so Mattie, his twice-a-week house keeper, was employed to stay with him at night. It was the same conspiracy that got rid of the Mercury Cougar—they did not trust him to drive. I was not sure if such tyranny was the cause of the hurt puppy look I saw in his eyes or if it was because he did not feel well. I could not fault his family for wanting to see that he was safe, but all their good intentions were clearly having an ill effect on William's quality of life. He wasn't very happy with things.

After the Seale lecture, Paul broke into a discussion of the savings and loans crisis of '87 and how greed would be the down fall of a great nation. He interrupted himself to recommend and then insist that I let the dogs out for a personal break. I pulled behind an old white church that was almost hidden from the highway and let the dogs out on a lead one at a time. Meanwhile Paul busied about reading the inscriptions on the cemetery markers next to the church. By and by we were reloaded and Paul launched into an observation about the names on the markers he had examined. "You don't often see the name 'Larkin,'" he began. "Not as a last name . . ."

"I'll tell you what is different this time," I interrupted, only half aware that we were in our own worlds of thought and that Paul had no idea that I was feeling deeply uneasy. He only looked at me. "This is the first time that we did not bring Leukos with us. But he has gotten too feeble, doesn't have any strength in his hind quarters and can hardly get up when he lies down. He has also gotten deaf as a rock and doesn't even act like he wants to go hunting. It makes me sad in a way, just thinking about old dogs, and old bird hunters." I laughed as if I had said something funny. Paul didn't laugh.

"What's different," he said almost under his breath, "is that this is likely to be our last hunt in Early County."

"Yeah, we said that as we left home, and I'm afraid so." Again there was silence, the silence of thought. "You know, Paul," I said, trying to clarify what I was thinking, "its like Coach Lions said many years ago: when you are young, you make a lot of friends, but when you are old, you make lots of acquaintances. I don't know if that was original with him or not, but my experience confirms that he was right."

"Yeah?" It was clear that I left something out of my rumination.

"Well, I was thinking about ole Leukos. He was loyal, long-suffering, always wanting to go where I went, never complained, never held a grudge even when I had buzzed him with the shock collar, and never wanted much more than to be what God created him to be—a bird dog. And in the thirteen years that I've had him, he's been a friend, a damned good friend. Although human and dog friendship may not be the same as human and human friendship, for the most part he did a much better job, present company excepted, of course."

"Of course."

"Now that he is old and can't hunt, I don't consider him useless; he is still a friend, and I feel I have an obligation to look after my friend as long as he lives. He would me if the shoe was on the other foot, and if he could. The point is that humans don't always feel the same when it comes to their human friends. I was wondering, maybe worrying about William—no children, no wife, and now not even a blessed dog!"

There was little additional conversation until we pulled into William's back yard. Immediately the back door swung open, and our host eased down the two steps into the carport grinning and chuckling the same as ever. He turned to say something to Toby who followed him into the carport, pointed to the Yukon, and the two burst into laughter. I couldn't make out the punch line, but it had something to do with bussing dogs or the like. It was a relief to see William laughing.

"I'm not hen-pecked, I promise, but Ruthie Mae just wouldn't let me bring her 'puppies' in the truck, not in this weather." My explanation added to the mirth.

"Hell, Doc," smiled William. "She probably still remembers the first time you took ole Leukos home with all those cockleburs."

"She does. God blessed her with total recall and perfect hindsight. She reminded me of that before we left home. But even Paul admits that she was right about bringing the Yukon, except for the farting."

There was another wrawl of laughter. All seemed ok, at least for the moment.

It wasn't long before we were again loaded on Toby's Kawasaki Mule. William was wearing a heavy hunting coat and a cap with ear flaps. Paul and I brought our jackets but shoved them into the storage area under the seat. I got a little chilly on the ride to the first let down and wondered if William was ok.

It was a lovely day for bird hunting in South Georgia. The rain had washed the air clear and bright, and the front had passed leaving it crisp and cool. The grass was still damp, and puddles persisted in tire tracks and low spots.

The first round we made was near Toby's house. We hunted a grass field that had been planted in pine a couple of months earlier. We found some birds, but one of the dogs put them up before we were in range. We had no luck with the singles and made our way back to the Mule to report the happenings to William and Toby. There was a constant breeze, but Paul and I were rather warm having walked through the tangles of tall grass and briar, each of us wearing only a heavy shirt and a hunting vest. As we approached the Mule we could see that William was bundled up, obviously cold. He had my heavy Filson coat over his lap and knees like a blanket and had Paul's jacket backward over his chest and shoulders. It was clearly Toby's work.

"The Doc and I worked up a sweat, William," Paul began as we approached, "but you look like you are about to freeze." In fact, he looked miserable.

"Let's go to the house and have a cup of coffee. Maybe tomorrow will be a better day." I suggested. No one disagreed.

Once we settled back at William's and were sitting around the oak kitchen table as we had many times previously, it became obvious to me that he was not well. He laughed less, coughed more. His cheeks were red and flushed, but there was paleness around his eyes and over his forehead. More worrisome than that, there was no sparkle in his blue eyes, no lilt in his voice. I tried several times to breach the subject of his health and what had transpired since the summer, but it became obvious that he did not want to talk about it. On one occasion when only the two of us were at the table he looked at me with a real sadness in his eyes and asked, "Doc, how about your health?" I replied that it was "ok." He then asked, "How about that prostate cancer? You've had it quite a while, haven't you?"

"It's doing ok. It's been like moss on a tree, so far. It's there but not doing any harm."

We each took sips at our coffee, and there was a long silence. I could see his eyes getting moist. "So far," he repeated. "That's good. I worry about you, Doc." There was something in my throat that kept me from replying.

It had been twelve years since my surgery, and the five that I had prognosticated for myself had more than doubled. The only thing that showed I had cancer was a blood test, a number—a stupid number. Though I was reminded every day by my hurt bladder and its urgency that I had been wounded, the thought of my mortality was not a front page issue in my mind, not usually. Knowing William's concern for me made me feel hypocritical, and I felt guilty for being so full of myself. I had attempted to inquire of his state of health, and he had turned it back on me. It was evident to me as a physician that his ailment was much more pernicious than mine. I realized also that his refusal to allow me to inquire about it was not pushing me away so much as it was his reluctance to bring it out and look at it; and that was ok, because as a friend I knew all that I needed to know.

That evening we went to the mullet house for supper. Toby drank a beer; Paul, William and I had tea. We all ate fried flounder and onion rings and cole slaw. We talked about past trips and laughed some, but I had difficulty looking anyone eye to eye. I knew not to.

Paul and I checked into the Days Inn south of Blakely. The manager, obviously Indian, lived in an apartment behind the office. The whole place smelled of curry, or some other spice, but was not unpleasant.

I took each of the dogs out and fed them, watered them and walked them about before bedding them down in the Yukon, letting the windows down as far as I dared. None of them was particularly tired since we had not hunted long, but each peacefully obeyed my whispered requests, and seemed to sense that there was something nostalgic, even spiritual about the night. I gave each one a few strokes on the ear and headed back to the motel room. The night was after-rain fresh and getting cool. The half moon was unusually bright it seemed, and stars were myriad. As I gazed up, thinking about the infinity that lay beyond what I could see, I could imagine the Psalmist singing:

> *". . . As for man, his days are as grass:*
> *As a flower of the field, so he flourisheth.*
> *For the wind passeth over it, and it is gone;*
> *And the place thereof shall know it no more."*

The morning came clear, and frost lay heavy on the Yukon and on the yards around the motel. We stopped at the shop-and-fill Toby had recommended and picked up breakfast for the four of us, mostly biscuits with ham or sausage or eggs and bacon. Though it smelled delicious, we did not partake until we had arrived at William's. We let out the dogs and joined William and Toby, who were at the table drinking coffee and taking about turkey hunting. William was jovial and seemed much more his old self. The conversation warmed as did the morning, and the biscuits vanished like the frost on the barn roof and the fields.

"Now Paul," began William, sounding familiar and whole, "you and Doc didn't order any special room service down at the motel, did you?"

"Like what?"

"Like one of Blakely's finest; like what I've been trying to get you lined up with every time you come down?"

"Be nice, William."

I could see a hint of the old sparkle in William's eyes again as he resumed his old game of pestering Paul. Occasionally he would attempt to draw me into it with, "Tell the truth, Doc. What did you and Paul really do last night?"

We waited until the morning had sufficiently warmed and felt almost spring-like before beginning the morning hunt. This time we hunted from Toby's crew cab Chevy truck. William delighted in the comfort and command of riding in the truck, and for much of the time he drove while Toby hunted with us. It was a good day, sunny and shirt-sleeve cool. The paper whites were blooming, and even a few daffodils were teasing with peeks of bright yellow.

We stopped by Toby's place mid afternoon to take a break and to see the new puppy his brother, Woody, had given him. As we drove up, the front door flew open and running out came the puppy and two squealing children, Bailey, six, and Alex, three. It was clear they were delighted to see their dad, rushing into his arms as he knelt down. They were immediately joined by the ten week old pointer puppy jumping and licking at their faces. What a scene of pure unbridled joy! I had seen it played out much the same with my own children and, in recent years, with my grandchildren. We relished the moment, the memories and the ambience of approaching spring.

As I opened the truck door, I turned and glanced up and whispered, "Thanks!"

"Amen!" Paul said out loud with a side glance at me. And we were off again to hunt birds.

My memory is not clear on how many coveys we found or how many birds we bagged. I do recall one covey the dogs pointed beside an old church yard in a privet thicket that struggled and thrashed to escape the tangle and then scattered in all directions. None of us fired a shot. We each asked almost in unison, "Why didn't *you* shoot?" It was ammunition for William's commentary the rest of the day.

The summer was hot and humid in Central Alabama that year, worse than usual it seemed. The weather report on WBRC had predicted another four days of high humidity and sweltering heat; old folks should stay in except early morning and late afternoon. I knew that this applied to me and was glad I had to work and that my office and the hospital were cool. "Thank God for Westinghouse!" I muttered out loud as I walked from my office across the parking lot to the back entrance of the hospital.

I disliked hospital meetings and especially called meetings of the Executive Committee. They are never pleasant, and when the problem is a disruptive physician, one who explodes in anger and curses and shouts at nurses and orderlies, it is a miserable experience. The outcome of the formally arranged gathering made no one happy, as predicted. Afterward I was too unsettled to eat lunch so instead fetched a cup of coffee and joined a fellow committeeman at a corner table, away from everyone else. "Why do some people have to be such assholes?" I asked as I sat down.

Not looking up from his tray, he replied, "Because that is just the way some people are. It's the same in every profession, I'll bet."

"Yeah? Well, I bet there has never been an executive committee of automobile dealers sending off some used car salesman to the shrink because he cusses out the mechanics and tire changers. Hell, it seems to me that medical education turns some of us prima donnas into sociopaths, pampas pricks and bombastic assholes. I have had enough of these confrontations to last me a life time. I feel like Jeremiah: just wish I had a traveler's lodging place in the desert where I could get away from these sinners, damned generation of vipers!"

"Just wait till quail season, and you can go to South Georgia and get all this off your mind a while."

"Yeah. That's for sure!"

I could not go to sleep that night for thinking on the events of the day and how it would be nice to escape from more of the same. Dwelling on unpleasant things doesn't help; I learned that a long time ago. And so thinking, I could not constrain a feeling of gratitude to the Almighty for allowing me to get lost in bird hunting on occasion. I thanked Him for that and for dogs and the tranquility of friendship.

The jingling of the phone interrupted my expression of thanksgiving. It was Paul, saying that he had talked to Toby, who reported that William had another spell, this one worse than before. When he got out of the hospital he would be going to a nursing home for several weeks, and maybe home after that, if he got a lot better.

William never got better. His neurological and intellectual functions agonizingly worsened by degree, slowly, gradually. The arthritic problem and its cumulative deformities and malfunctions with which he had contended all his life, those things which took a dogged effort to keep him functional were overcoming his purposeful determination. His will to hold on was dissipating as was the other stuff that made him who he was. Paul, Toby and I visited him in the nursing home several weeks later. None of us said "good by," not out loud. None of us said much of anything; I certainly didn't for fear that it would commence too much emotion, maybe even tears. I tried to remain as stolid as possible, though I'm not sure why. It just seemed better to be superficial, but below the surface lay a torrent of feeling, of unspeakable sadness. Driving home Paul and I hardly spoke, our thoughts too deep and too private to make room for trivial conversation. I kept thinking about how as a physician I had always tried to follow the admonition of Sir William Osler and maintain an air of imperturbability and equanimity in bad situations. I wondered if it was really applicable in this situation. I wanted to cry. My mind kept returning to the Psalmist, *"But the mercy of the Lord,"* he sang, *"is from everlasting to everlasting."*

William died in May and was buried in the Blakely City Cemetery. Paul and I returned for the funeral which was only grave side. I don't know why it was that way. At first it seemed too little for him, but then again, that's probably the way he wanted it.

XI

Sunset

Both of us felt that it was our duty, and it was our desire, to go to William's funeral. While his death brought about a profound sadness, it was not a tragic event. He had suffered some, and he had lingered and dissipated longer than he would have wanted, so at some level his death was a relief. It was a relief in much the same way that Leukos' death had been a relief. It was different on the same scale that the life of a human is different from that of a dog, but admittedly when I consider how they each died, I am struck that the feelings were so similar. I had witnessed both as they progressively deteriorated physically and mentally, neither apparently aware that they were slipping into the realm of the infinite. The life they enjoyed had long since gone, however gradually. I grieved their decline more than their deaths and reflecting, dreaded worse my own declivity and feared less my demise. Tears, too, brought some sense of closure. It seemed appropriate to cry: I loved them both. For Paul and me the drive to Early County was not morbid or lugubrious, but we didn't talk much; we didn't have to.

We knew some of the folks at the funeral. Toby and his family were there, as were William's brother and two of his sisters and their flocks. His sister, the one who had lived in our town, was not there. She was in a nursing home in Athens, victim of the ravages of Alzheimer's disease. We met William's lady friend, the one who baked pound cakes and who borrowed the butcher knife and lived in Fort Gaines. She was very pleasant and was anxious to meet us because she had heard all the stories from William and felt that she knew us.

The service was simple and brief, the way William would have wanted. It was only grave side, no church service. A couple of hymns were sung, some words said, and prayer. The May sun was hot at 2:00 o'clock, and my dark suit soaked up its rays like a black top road in July. There wasn't much shade, and the wind lay quiet as if holding its breath. I could not tell if it was tears or sweat that I blotted with the folded paper towel I kept in the back pants pocket. I turned away from the family seated under the tent, the preacher, the funeral directors, and the coffin suspended over the grave, and I grieved—silently, I think—for the end of a friendship, the end of an era, and for whatever was causing the sadness. There is something about friendship that is much more than deference, more than respect or even reverence; it is a gift to be venerated, to be cherished and loved. It is so brief, so transient, so to be enjoyed while it is present!

"Let me tell you something sad—and strange," I said to Paul as we headed back toward home. "I was standing around introducing myself to William's family and making small talk when I overheard a conversation two of them were having. One of them said, 'He was one sombich who had it made: never worked a day in his life.' Hell, I couldn't believe it!"

"Why'd he say that?"

"I haven't a clue. Surely he didn't mean it. Surely not! Maybe it was some sort of joke."

"Well, let me tell you something *really* sad, and this will kill you." I waited for Paul to continue. "Toby told me that someone had shot Denver and the little pointer puppy."

"No way!"

"Yes. He found them on the side of the road about half a mile from his house. Thinks he knows who did it, but can't be sure."

"Oh, Gee! Those kids loved that puppy, and Denver was always with Toby. That's awful, just awful! I think I'd want to hurt someone who did that to my dogs."

"It wouldn't bring 'em back."

"I'm just saying how I would feel." What I felt was anger and contempt for any one who would hurt a dog, especially a neighbor's dog, and especially one who was the source of joy for those children. And the uneasy, sorrowful feeling that gnawed at the raw part of my emotion was replaced for a moment with rancor.

It was the fourth year since I had come into possession of 400 acres in Coosa County, only eight miles from home. It was a fluke the way it happened, almost as if directed by the hand of God. I had owned some land on the other side of town for twenty-five years and had considered it of not much value. It could hardly have been used for much because a two-tower power transmission line and a gas pipe line crossed there and precluded development. I tried on several occasions to sell the place but was never successful. With deregulation of the power industry there developed a keen interest in rural property where these utilities crossed, making an ideal location for a gas generated power plant. I was made an offer that I could not resist and did a deal with a power company and set out to do a like-kind transfer for some property that joined our home place. At the eleventh hour the property swap fell through despite months of planning and bargaining. Rather than pocketing the filthy lucre, I found the Coosa County property and did a deal with the owner, all along thinking that I would find something more suitable later on.

As it turned out the Coosa property was a diamond in the rough. The out of state owner had taken little interest in it; consequently, it had been neglected for years and had been the victim of a clear cut timber operation a few years earlier. But it is amazing what fire can do to clean up such a mess, and four yearly prescribed burns did wonders for this land, converting the logging slash and hardwood resprout into an almost park like game habitat. We drained the old pond and stocked it with bream and bass. The old double pen cabin with the chimneys fallen down was restored to its 1900's condition, and the old rock lined well was reclaimed. It was a great project, one that brought tremendous satisfaction, especially in the spring when the bobwhites called.

This property is adjacent to a small ancient church, Friendship Methodist Church, a picturesque white country church with a tall, narrow, cross-topped steeple, which we can see clearly from our hills a mile away. Naturally, we call the Coosa property 'Friendship.' That name is fitting in many ways.

The native quail population improved but not to the point it could tolerate much hunting pressure. To get around this I tried releasing birds at feeders in October, letting them adopt for a month before hunting them. I found that barrel feeders with motorized distributors worked ok, and that those birds that survived the first month's predation provided good game. By December the birds acted and flew like wild birds, as long as they were provided food. It took the pressure off the wild birds and was a good substitute for sure enough bird hunting, although not the same, not really.

I called Toby in December and suggested that he come for a look see and hunt. Toby owned a small plane and flew up one morning before Christmas. I met him at the airport, and we dropped by the house to get the dogs and for Ruth to meet him. She was not disappointed. Toby was the age of our oldest son, Bill, and they were very much alike—youthful good looks, intelligent, nice smile, generous with complements, and loquacious. Ruth, who also does not lack for conversation, was most engaging and charming as usual. She inquired of Toby's wife and children, of whom she had received numerous reports. The schmoozing grew increasingly thick and sticky, so I suggested we proceed to Friendship for fear Ruth might induct him into our family as an honorary son, or knight him as the Sublime Prince of the Piper Cub and Protector of the Frail Elderly Patriarch.

It was a good day. We found several coveys, and all the birds flew well. We hunted the old fashioned way, walking the entire time. This was a change for Toby, but he did not complain. In contrast I whined and whimpered about the discomfort of plantar fasciitis which had plagued me all season. At mid-day Ruth met us at the cabin with barbeque sandwiches and iced tea, and conversation. She gave Toby the grand tour of the cabin, and before leaving even explained to him that her name was not Ruthie Mae as I was want to call her.

"Some people have it made," he observed as she drove away. "The wife waits on him hand and foot, and even brings him lunch when he is off bird hunting."

"Yeah, you are right about having it made, my naïve and youthful companion, but you do not understand that if I were here hunting alone, I would not be eating barbeque."

In late February, Toby called and invited Paul and me to hunt with him at his brother's plantation down near Colquitt, Georgia, a few miles south of Blakely. It was Toby's way of keeping the 'William tradition' going, and we were quick to accept the invitation. We planned to hunt Friday and to stay at the same motel we had stayed in the last time we hunted with him and William, and we planned to hunt till mid-day on Saturday. Still suffering from plantar fasciitis, made much worse by the day-long hunt Toby and I had made a few weeks earlier, I was uncertain about a lot of walking.

On Thursday we went to the Russell Outlet Store and picked up some Auburn tee-shirts and caps for Bailey and Alex, and we were pleased the next day at the delight they took in the gifts. Children are easily pleased by surprises, and they grow and change effortlessly, almost magically, especially to the eyes that only see them on occasion. It is interesting how age intensifies the delight one takes in children, especially grandchildren and the children of one's friends. They are enthralled by simple things, become as excited as puppies, and are as pure as morning sunshine. Such were the pride of Toby and Brandi. Missing were Denver, the lab, and the pointer puppy. They had not been replaced.

The drive to Colquitt was interrupted by a side trip to inspect some property Toby and his brother, Woody, had recently purchased. It was flat land and much of it was a large swamp. Toby pointed out a couple of 'pet' alligators that lay along the debris at the edge of the dark water. "You put your dogs out near here, Doc John, and they might not go home with you."

"If they don't go home, I can't," I observed. "Let's go somewhere else to hunt."

Woody is two years older than Toby. He is pleasant and talkative like his brother, and their voices are so much alike that if one closed his eyes it would be difficult to tell which was talking. The similarity ended there. Woody is chubby and balding and a little more reserved than Toby.

We were hunting with my dogs, the three who were born of Leukos and Belle. The two male setters were large dogs and mostly white like their sire. I called them "The White Boys" when I hunted them together. Mae was much smaller, less than half their size, and looked remarkably like a Brittany spaniel. All the dogs ran loose at home, but unlike the two males, she was constantly on the move, always hunting. She was overactive to a fault and, as our vet observed, "crazy." She had a good nose but was bad to blink and to flush birds, probably in part because of her solitary hunting. It was best to hunt her alone and remind her from time to time about the electronic collar, and the need to constrain her impulses.

Mae found the first covey, which she predictably flushed before we could get close. Fortunately it was a large covey, so we were able to find a number of singles. She was content to locate the downed birds and to pick them up as if keeping count but flat refused to retrieve. The White Boys did better, and we had a successful hunt, even finding some pen-raised birds left over from the previous day's release hunt. But it was not the same, not without William.

Come mid March and turkey season, before the greening of outdoors, the thrill of turkey hunting lured me out of bed before daylight. I was able on one particular occasion to be up in time to settle with my back against a huge white oak before daylight and listen as the sky lightened in the east for the first gobble. I could always count on it coming from a grove of ancient pine cloistered on the east side of the hard wood hill a quarter mile from the house. I put out all my gear the night before and quickly slipped out of the house without waking Ruth. The bird dogs had chosen to sleep in the laundry room that night, so I eased out the side door, not even disturbing Sludge who was asleep on the couch.

I had been sitting only five minutes, and had been awake less than thirty, when Daddy Red Snout sounded a thundering gobble not a hundred yards in front of me. After a few seconds, I did a soft yelp with the cedar box, and he immediately gobbled back, saying that he was coming. The ruffle of feathers on heavy wings as he flew down caused my heart to pound, and my breath to become short. I purred softly with the cedar box and put it down, resting the barrel of the Remington 1100 on my right knee, pulling the butt tight against my shoulder. I could feel the blood thumping in my index finger as it rested on the safety. The sound of my heart throbbing in my ears became inseparable from the ever so gradual crescendo of the drumming bird as he marched toward my oak. I could see him at seventy yards and was sure that he could see me. There was not even a leaf between us, but he was coming, determined and strutting. Then at fifty yards, he stopped. His body thinned and his head shot up like a periscope, his wattle blazing red. I did not breathe. For minutes he just stood there out of range, a shotgun pointed at his head. "Come on!" I said to myself. But he was frozen, silent, suspicious, knowing that the camouflaged blob at the base of the oak was not supposed to be there. He knew something was not right. "Where is Ollie when I need him," I thought. Turkeys remind me of William. I'm sure he and Toby would have taken this one home.

Ruth had rearranged the ornaments on the Christmas tree several times that afternoon, and I had made myself as scarce as possible so as to avoid the tedium. The late afternoon was winter cold, and as I was fetching one more stick of fire wood, the phone rang.

It was a surprise to hear Toby's voice. "Doc John, This is Toby."

"Toby! What a surprise!"

"How are doing, Doc John?"

"Like a young mule! How are things with you?" I was delighted to hear from him, and I'm sure I sounded ebullient.

"Not so good. Not at all." I sensed distress and more in his voice.

"What's wrong, Toby?"

"Several weeks ago Bailey got sick. At first we thought she had a cold, but when she didn't get any better we took her to the doctor. He said she had acute leukemia . . ." there was a slight pause.

"Oh, Toby . . ."

"And, uh, Doc John, we took her up to Birmingham to Children's Hospital . . ."

"That's a good place for her to be," I interrupted.

"They gave her some chemotherapy and it seemed to be working, but her platelet count went down real bad. And, Doc John, she bled . . . had a stroke. Bled in her brain. They had to put her on life support."

"Oh, Dear God! No! Toby, I'm so . . ." I choked and my throat closed.

"That was a week ago. We took her off the respirator this morning." There was silence, and then he continued. "We are nearly home now, and I just wanted you and Mr. Paul to know.

"I don't know what to say, Toby. I'm so, so sorry." I got out only a squeaky whisper and tried not to sob in the phone.

"I just wanted you to know. That's all. I had wanted to call you all along, but couldn't do it. I can't talk, Doc John."

"I'll call Paul. We will see you at the service. Thanks for letting us know."

It must have been a difficult thing to call a friend and report that your child had died. I cannot even begin to imagine how difficult it must have been; but compared to *watching* your child die . . . I had witnessed such tragedy before, many times as an oncologist, many times, also, because I am old and am a man and live among men.

We attended Bailey's funeral. What an intense sadness! There were a myriad unconsoled tears and agonizing sobs. At the cemetery, after the crowd thinned, we hugged and said words.

Heading west from Georgia we drove in silence thinking of the sorrow of the day, squinting through tear-washed eyes toward the burning sun. Struggling, dying, finally setting, its rays refracted in the atmosphere and beaconed through the stratus clouds creating brilliant reds and silvers. Never had I seen so bright a sky at sunset, or such blazing, robust red! Red like the roses on the casket, or the rims of her mother's eyes: red like the sobs and the heart break! It seemed that the accumulated grief was glowing like an ember in the darkening sky, too bright and too intense to look upon. "Dear God!" I thought, "It is the Bailey sunset!"

There are good and happy memories of Early County Georgia, each more precious because of the contrasting price life demands. One can count life by minutes and years; but it is better, I conclude, to count life by friends and family, by dogs and quail, and long remembered covey rises, and cold days. But especially friends! You can say that nothing lasts forever, but I'm not so sure; I want to believe that some things do.

Get Published, Inc!
Thorofare, NJ 08086
04 November 2009
BA2009247